Jean Genet

Revised Edition

Twayne's World Authors Series

French Literature

David O'Connell, Editor

Georgia State University

TWAS 44

JEAN GENET
(1910–1986)

Photograph by Jerry Bauer.

Jean Genet

Revised Edition

By Bettina L. Knapp

Hunter College and the Graduate Center of the City University of New York

Twayne Publishers
A Division of G. K. Hall & Co. • Boston

To my husband

Jean Genet, Revised Edition
Bettina L. Knapp

Published by Twayne Publishers
A Division of G. K. Hall & Co.
70 Lincoln Street
Boston, Massachusetts 02111

Copyediting supervised by Barbara Sutton.
Book publication by Janet Zietowski.
Book design by Barbara Anderson.

Typeset in 11 pt. Garamond
by Huron Valley Graphics, Inc., Ann Arbor, Michigan.

Printed on permanent/durable acid-free paper
and bound in the United States of America.

Library of Congress Cataloging-in-Publication Data

Knapp, Bettina Liebowitz, 1926–
Jean Genet / by Bettina L. Knapp. — Rev. ed.
p. cm. — (Twayne's world authors series ; TWAS 44. French literature)
Bibliography: p.
Includes index.
ISBN 0-8057-8240-0 (alk. paper)
1. Genet, Jean, 1910– —Criticism and interpretation.
I. Title. II. Series: Twayne's world authors series ; TWAS 44.
III. Series: Twayne's world authors series. French literature.
PQ2613.E53Z76 1989
848′.91209—dc19 88-21308
CIP

Contents

About the Author

Bettina L. Knapp received her B.A. from Barnard College and her M.A. and Ph.D. from Columbia University and has studied at the Sorbonne. She is professor of French and comparative literatures at Hunter College and the Graduate Center of the City University of New York. She has received a Guggenheim Fellowship and awards from the American Philosophical Society, the Research Foundation of the City University of New York, and the Shuster Fund. She is a member of PEN and was named officer of the Order of Palmes Académiques by the French government.

Knapp is the author of numerous works, including *Louis Jouvet, Man of the Theatre; Gérard de Nerval, the Mystic's Dilemma; Antonin Artaud, Man of Vision; A Jungian Approach to Literature; Archetype, Architecture, and the Writer; Music, Archetype, and the Writer;* and *Women in Twentieth-Century Literature.* Also for the Twayne World Authors Series, she has written *Jean Cocteau* and *Jean Cocteau, Updated Edition; George Duhamel; Maurice Maeterlinck; Sacha Guitry,* and *Fernand Crommelynck.*

Preface

Reading Jean Genet's works is like being thrust into a labyrinth or like seeking a footing on quicksand. His characters are complex, ambiguous, and continually dissolving into one another. At times they are identifiable human beings; at others they are grotesque shadows. Events are described elusively, the real and the illusory overlapping each other. These, together with the effulgent sensuality of Genet's prose, the hypnotic cadences of his sentences, and the violence of his metaphors involve the reader emotionally and viscerally, but intellectually or rationally leave him struggling.

Genet's characters and the events in which they participate have emotionally human, rational, and recognizable aspects. This is especially the case when they are reflections of Genet's own life. In this volume I analyze these aspects as well as Genet's writings. But there is another quality present in Genet's works that is impersonal, inhuman, and mysterious. It is this side of his creative writings, expressions, and elaborations of the deepest layers within him that I also tried to fathom.

Genet's works guided me. He wrote that the author's role is "to point out the universal in a specific phenomenon." There, it seemed to me, lies the key: to interpret and analyze the myths, images, symbols, visions, rituals, dreams, and motifs that Genet recounted in his works, from a broad and universal point of view as well as from a specific and personal standpoint.

In Genet's first novel, *Our Lady of the Roses,* I noticed, for example, its mythical aspects: how the ancient Medea-like female figure emerged, in her most vicious form, as a son killer, and how her dread presence filled the atmosphere with hate. In the play *The Blacks,* this same mythical female force was put to positive use to show the victory of a matriarchal society over a patriarchal one. In the novel *Quarrel of Brest,* I wondered why and how a murderer was reliving the ancient myth of sin, sacrifice, and resurrection. I discovered that this myth, as experienced by Genet's hero, revealed, symbolically speaking, his inner growth, his emotional liberation from his environment and from his anxieties; and strangely enough, since Genet's heroes are "extensions" of himself, it reflected a literary change in the author's works. It was after the completion of *Quarrel of Brest* that Genet began writing plays.

A study of Genet's imagery, which is an intrinsic part of his work, was also undertaken in an effort to determine why, for example, images such as glass, windows (*Our Lady of the Flowers*), balconies (*The Balcony*), screens (*The Screens*), fountains, ships, and birds (*Miracle of the Rose*) are so frequently used. Studied in context, these images become visual transpositions of inner mental states and reveal facets of the characters' personalities and philosophies that might otherwise have remained incomprehensible.

The types of people Genet described in his works, the acts and events recounted, are treated symbolically and in their broad sense. The criminal, for example, is understood by Genet as being a man of *action;* the crime, as an *act.* In this connection, Adam comes to mind. In that he rebelled against God, he committed a negative act; in that he brought man the fruit of knowledge, his act was a positive one. Genet's heroes, in one respect or another, follow this same pattern. The murderer Lefranc (*Deathwatch*), comparable to Cain in certain respects, is not killed, nor is his biblical counterpart. Why? Symbolically speaking, the criminal serves two functions in society: the negative one of destroying established traditions and laws; the positive one of being a virulent force that provides society with the stimulation and energy necessary to renew and reactivate what might otherwise stagnate.

Visions also figure in Genet's works. The narrator's vision, for example, in the *Miracle of the Rose,* provokes a religious experience that results in his gaining *new* sight or expanded consciousness. Upon his return to the world of reality, the narrator realizes that his future lies not in an *outward* search, but rather in an inward one: that the stuff from his creative works would be molded henceforth, would be carved out of himself.

Prayers, incantations, worship of the phallus as rituals that provoke mystic experiences are replete in Genet's works. To these rituals he adds others that serve divinity: the cult of the assassin from which a divinely inspired act results; prostitution, a form of phallic worship; and war, the criminal act par excellence. A study of these rituals and the mystical experiences that ensue enabled me to understand why certain of Genet's heroes longed to lose whatever identity they had and be absorbed into the collective, the same feeling that overcomes a parishioner in a house of worship.

Dreams described in Genet's works are also analyzed in order to delve more deeply into the meaning of the works under consideration. One of the most significant dreams is recounted in the *Mirale of the Rose.* The narrator dreams that he is on a ship, that he is climbing the cross-shaped mast, that he slips and falls into the arms of the captain. Such a dream, in brief, expresses a veritable *imitatio Christi,* the narrator's overly spiritual attitude that is impossible for a human to bear. The narrator, therefore, falls from the mast indicating that he has dropped into the opposite extreme—an overly instinctual attitude. Such conflicts (as expressed through varying altitudes) are a pictorial indication of an abstract inner imbalance experienced by the dreamer. He is, so to speak, poles apart from himself. If he does not want to be forever juggled from one point of view to another, if he wants to find his way in life, the dream indicates that he will have to take stock of himself, which he does in the course of the narrative.

The feeling of duality and fragmentation in all of Genet's protagonists and by extension in the author himself, is intensified by their longing for the opposite: unity, wholeness, the universal—God. Genet's works embrace every religion from the most ancient to the most modern. He sees God in every phase of existence. Not the limited God, however, worshiped by those adhering to organized religions, but an infinite, transpersonal deity imbedded in all regions of the cosmos. Genet's extreme involvement with God is not only revealed through the shattering mystical experiences in the *Miracle of the Rose* and in *Quarrel of Brest,* but is also apparent in what he calls his "pilgrimage," which he recounts in *The Thief's Journal,* and in his nature descriptions in which God is revealed in his infinite manifestations.

Genet's prose is poetry. Its musicality, its inner rhythms and cadences, spontaneous, but at times, paradoxically enough, studied, are in many ways reminiscent of the works of Jean-Jacques Rousseau. The visual images so important to Genet in bringing forth his feelings sometimes have the sculptural effects and color contents of the poems of Théophile Gautier. The violent and the sardonic language reveal affinities with Rimbaud and Lautréamont; the sensuality, with Baudelaire.

Bettina L. Knapp

Hunter College and the Graduate Center of CUNY

Chronology

1910 Jean Genet born illegitimately in Paris, 19 December; abandoned by his mother; becomes ward of the National Foundling Society. Lives in the Morvan region of France with foster parents.

1920 Begins to steal. Sent to Mettray Reformatory.

1926 Escapes from Mettray. Joins Foreign Legion and deserts.

1932–1940 Travels through Spain, Italy, Albania, Yugoslavia, Austria, Poland, Czechoslovakia, Germany, Belgium, and France.

1942 Sent to Fresnes Prison upon his return to France. Writes first novel, *Notre-Dame-des-Fleurs.*

1943 In La Santé and Tourelles prisons. Writes the novel *Miracle de la Rose.*

1944 *Notre-Dame-des-Fleurs,* published.

1946 *Miracle de la Rose* published.

1947 *Pompes funèbres* and *Querelle de Brest,* novels, published. *Les Bonnes,* play, performed.

1948 *Journal du voleur,* biography, published. Released from prison on presidential pardon.

1949 *Haute Surveillance,* play, produced. *Adame Miroir,* ballet, published.

1956 *Le Balcon,* play, published.

1957 *Le Balcon* performed in London.

1958 *Les Nègres,* play, and *L'Atelier d'Alberto Giacometti,* essay, published.

1959 *Les Nègres* performed.

1961 *Les Paravents,* play, published.

1965 *Les Paravents* performed.

1968 "Ce qui est resté d'un Rembrandt déchiré en petits carrés." Travels to United States and becomes associated with Black Panthers.

1970 Travels in United States speaking on behalf of Black Panthers and jailed Bobby Seale. "May Day Speech" at Yale University against the American government.

1971 Introduction to *Soledad Brothers: The Prison Letters* of George Jackson.

1973 Becomes militant supporter of the Palestinians. Travels in North Africa, Lebanon, and Jordan.

1977 Takes up the cause of Red Army, German anarchists. Writes introduction to prison letters of Ulrike Meinhof.

1981 Makes one-hour film, *Genet,* directed by Antoine Bourseiller.

1982 Rainer Werner Fassbinder's film *Quarrel.*

1986 Travels in Europe, England, and North Africa. Dies on 15 April. *L'Amoureux captif* published posthumously.

Part One

The Novel: Ascension through Degradation

A damned descending without lamp
To the edge of an abyss the odor of which
Betrays its humid depths,
Of eternal stairs without ramps
Where viscous monsters watch
Whose large phosphorus eyes
Make a night still darker
And render only them visible. . . .
—Charles Baudelaire, "The Irremediable,"
The Flowers of Evil

Chapter One
Genet's Life

Remember particularly that you cannot be a judge of any one. For no one can judge a criminal until he recognizes that he is just such a criminal as the man standing before him, and that he perhaps is more than all men to blame for that crime.

—Fyodor Dostoyevski, *The Brothers Karamazov*

The very paucity of information available concerning Jean Genet's life has triggered the imagination and curiosity of his readers. His wish for secrecy, however, has been respected by his friends and admirers. That few new facts have been revealed over the years concerning Genet's private world has added to the mythic dimension of his existence and his works. Indeed, it may be said that Genet, the creator of myths, has been transformed into one.

Jean Genet was born on 19 December 1910. He was given his birth certificate, he tells us in *Journal du voleur* (*The Thief's Journal*), twenty-one years later. From it he learned that he had been born in Paris at 22 rue d'Assas, behind the Luxembourg Gardens. He went to Paris hoping to get some sort of information about his family background. He discovered only that his father's name was unknown, that his mother had called herself Gabrielle Genet, and that the address indicated on the birth certificate was a maternity hospital. The rest of his genealogy was and is shrouded in mystery.

Genet spent his early years as a ward of the National Foundling Society, which later paid a peasant family in the Morvan region of France, north of the Massif Central to keep him and bring him up.

The Morvan is a rainy region, thickly forested with mountainous areas, plateaus, rivers, and plains. Cattle breeding, the wood-products industry, and fishing have through the years become the chief source of income for the inhabitants of this district. Its cities, such as Château-Chinon, Avallon, and Saulieu, are little more than giant markets with a backdrop of medieval history. Here the young orphan spent his early years and learned to familiarize himself with nature, both its active and passive aspects. Living close to the land, he drew from it strength and understanding.

Judging from his later writings, it would seem that Genet was an introverted child who experienced a rich and vibrant imaginative life. He lived one life on the outside, another on the inside. A good, docile child working well in school and going to church regularly was the face society knew; beneath the mask smoldered another personality. Alone most of the time, fundamentally alien to his peasant family, he frequently invented a family, preferably of royal blood, that doted on him alone. At times he would consider nature his family: the giant trees and wind-swept flowers bowing to him as he walked along. He tried to communicate with plants, the sun, and the moon; to decipher nature's languages. He discovered that nature reflected and answered his moods. Society, on the other hand, represented a threat, a danger. When lying in a field of gold in August, the young orphan felt himself disappearing, becoming a tree or a flower, merging and blending with his surroundings. As he watched the sun cross the sky, he responded to the fiery ball's inner luminescence, and, like the sun casting its shadow, the young Genet similarly watched his own shadow grow longer and longer. As the sun set and darkness fell upon him, he was captured by his own underworld with its dangers and frights, its traps and temptations—all those anxieties known to a boy thrust into a world without a thing of his own but his flesh and blood. At night his companions were the planets and stars; for brief moments he felt himself leaving the earth to join those "unknowns" inhabiting Uranus, to converse with the Dioscuri. The wind, the storms, thunder and lightning, the harsh forest sounds, the yelping of the animals being brought down from pasture were all externalizations of the emotions the boy was then experiencing. Genet was a primitive in that he responded instinctively and directly to the forces of nature; he felt an affinity with them; he found "actuality" in them; they enabled him to discover the sources and roots that he needed so desperately.

It was at the age of ten, wrote Jean-Paul Sartre in his monumental work *Saint Genet,* that the young boy began to steal. According to Sartre, Genet had decided to be a thief at this juncture. His existential choice had been made. Genet himself, however, writing in *The Thief's Journal,* stated, "It was not at any precise period of my life that I decided to be a thief."[1] Whatever the interpretation may be, Jean Genet began to steal. He was chastised by the peasant family for his transgressions. He asked for their forgiveness and was pardoned until the next theft set off another round of accusations and expiations.

Finally, when it became impossible for the peasant family to curb his propensity for thievery, Genet was sent to Mettray Reformatory in the Loire region. Mettray at the time was considered a center for discipline and a "punitive model" for inculcating in its inmates "the art of power relations" through "the coercive technologies of behavior."[2] At Mettray Genet was indoctrinated into life. Far from the relatively staid atmosphere he had hitherto known living with his Morvan foster parents, he was thrust among a group of young hoodlums. Locked up, living under strict regulations, the orphan began slowly to become self-aware, to live out what he had only suspected was dormant within his character.

Later, in *The Thief's Journal,* his autobiography in a sense, Genet described his features, basing his verbal sketch on a prison photo: "My face is oval, very pure; my nose is smashed, flattened by a punch in some forgotten fight. The look on my face is blasé, sad, and warm, very serious. My hair was thick and unruly. Seeing myself at that age, I expressed my feelings almost aloud: "Poor little fellow, you've suffered' " (*TJ,* 85). Prison had a twofold effect on him: "Prison offered me the first consolation, the first peace, the first friendly fellowship: I experienced them in the realm of foulness. Much solitude had forced me to become my own companion" (*TJ,* 86). Confronted with his own wretchedness, solitude, and a sense of rejection, his resentment grew apace and parallel with a hatred that increased and fed his inner fire and violence: "Abandoned by my family, I already felt it was natural to aggravate this condition by a preference for boys, and this preference by theft, and theft by crime or a complacent attitude in regard to crime. I thus resolutely rejected a world which had rejected me" (*TJ,* 86).

Genet, criminal and now homosexual, escaped from Mettray and joined the French Foreign Legion, signing for a period of five years in order to collect a bonus for voluntary enlistment. He deserted after a few days, taking the suitcases of some black officers with him. Some months later he became a human Seeing Eye dog to the blind poet René de Buxeuil. Although Buxeuil's name has passed into oblivion, when Genet worked for him he was popular for his sentimental verses, his moralistic and religiously oriented ballads, and for the fact that he had been chosen by the Camelots du Roi, the right-wing royalist legion, to compose their marching song.

When in Buxeuil's employ in 1926 Genet began to amuse himself by writing songs, but routine was not to his liking, and once again he took to the tramp's existence, thieving as he wandered. In 1930, when he was twenty, he wrote his first poem. No longer extant, the poem was about a little girl whom he had loved and who had died at the age of ten.

Genet was a loner. During these years, he had developed a composite of opposites within himself: aggression and helplessness; activity and passivity; a thirst for revenge and a sense of hurt, dissatisfaction, and satisfaction; spirituality and sensuality; anger and nostalgia. He dreamed of becoming a figure of importance, of overcoming the prosaic dimensions of the petty criminal. He wanted to be strong, hard, and formidable. He longed to be a killer like Pilorge or Weidmann, two guillotined criminals whom he had made into heroes and put on pedestals in his works. He dreamed of being dispatched to a penal colony in Guiana, of meeting his fate there in the blazing sun. But—in reality—he was not of a mold to become a lord of crime. He was a dwarf trying to destroy a mountain: society. The rejected one, therefore, must not only damage without (society), but hurt within (himself). He sought punishment, social ostracism, prison, or capital punishment with an inner joy. Like Herostratos, who, in order to earn both fame and punishment, burned the Temple of Artemis in Ephesus on the day Alexander the Great was born, so Genet, the criminal homosexual, wanted to prove by some grand *act* that he was not a helpless pawn, but, on the contrary, strong and virile. His unconscious feeling of inadequacy would thereby be overcome by the Herostratic act; expiation through punishment would be his.[3]

From 1932 to 1940 Genet attempted to prove his mettle: to become hard and strengthen himself against pain. He went on a *pilgrimage:* his goal was to reach the lowest possible state of *evil.* To become base, sordid, vile, degraded was his *credo,* his way. His would be an inner and downward journey into an abyss. For eight years he was to do *penance* by traveling and living with the dregs of humanity in Barcelona, France, Italy, Yugoslavia, Poland, Czechoslovakia, Belgium, and Nazi Germany. He became the most degenerate of degenerates, seeking his livelihood by begging, prostitution, and dope smuggling.

There are, however, conflicting reports as to how Genet proceeded on what he calls his "pilgrimage." An article by German writer and journalist Lily Pringsheim, who lived in Brno and who met Genet there late in 1937, describes Genet as a "rather undersized, indeed almost dainty, vagabond" who possessed "a truly astonishing intelligence and a quite remarkable talent." Pringsheim adds: "I could scarcely believe the extent of his knowledge of literature, since, except for a few short breathing spaces, he had been continually in jail. . . ." Seemingly, Genet visited Pringsheim many times in Brno, and when he remained overnight, he chose and was granted not a bed, but "a very narrow projecting ledge of a balcony." It gave him the opportunity of looking up at the stars, which he enjoyed doing, she noted. Because he was not accustomed to a bed, or to other normal comforts, he did not miss them. Nor did he ever have any luggage, wrote Therese, Pringsheim's daughter. He always wore the same brown corduroy suit and black turtleneck sweater for months on end. Accompanying him always, however, was "a cowhide folder full of manuscripts and writing materials."[4]

After spending several months in Brno, Czechoslovakia, and earning his living by giving private French lessons to the daughter of a well-known gynecologist, and probably to others as well, Genet went on to Katovice, Poland, where he was again sent to prison. Once freed, he traveled on to Berlin, Brussels, and Antwerp, finally arriving in Paris in late 1937, only to be sent back to prison for issuing forged passports and also as punishment for having deserted the French Foreign Legion.[5]

During Genet's *pilgrimage* he was in and out of jail from one end of Europe to another. He willed himself to march *down* and *down,* each time adding another vice to his already long list. He lived intimately with excrement; his byword was betrayal. The journey was to be bruising and arduous, and it left Genet more solitary than ever. Nothing was too low for him, as nothing was too low for Saint Marie Alacoque, "who gathered up the dejecta of sick persons with her tongue.[6] The rejected orphan had become a pariah. It was his turn now to consciously reject others. And he did just that: "I was an illegitimate child. I was outside the social order. What could I wish for, if not for a special destiny? . . . the only thing left for me was to want to be a saint, just that: in other words, a negation of man."[7]

Genet's odyssey is the story of one man's *ascension* through *degradation.* Nothing was spared him, and he let nothing escape him in the domain of human suffering. He turned himself inside out to lay his smudged, sickly, suffering soul bare for all to scorn and stone. It was society's angered reaction that he sought. He wanted hatred to be heaped upon him by society for his transgressions and his homosexuality; by his fellow criminals for his betrayals; and later, by his readers, for his pornography, insults, and deceptions. The emotions he was experiencing during his pilgrimage into the abyss later became the fundament and substance of his works of art.

Yet, wherever he was, whatever degradation he experienced, God *was always with him.* Genet wrote that he had "God in his guts." It became possible for him to know the numinous, the supernatural, the sacred aspects of life. Cut off from man, living in utter isolation, a pariah—he entered into communication with his *inner God*—his Self.

Each important experience at this point in his life took on a *sacred* aspect and became a *ceremony.* Thievery, for example, had become a *sacred ritual,* a moving mystical experience. Nothing illustrates this point better than what he revealed of himself in a Yugoslavian jail. Unable to speak the language of his cellmates, Genet felt even more isolated than ever and found it, therefore, still more arduous to earn their hatred. One afternoon, the inmates of his cell decided to play a game. They asked Genet to join them. The goal of the game was to pick the pocket of a sleeping convict without awakening him. Each prisoner tried his luck. There was no danger at all involved in this sport. When Genet's turn came to withdraw some objects from the sleeping prisoner's pocket, he fainted.

Genet fainted because his unconscious would not permit such a frivolous approach to an act that held such importance to him, although his conscious mind was quite unaware of this. Thieving was not a game, a pastime to be entered into freely and at will. To steal out of necessity, which is what Genet had done many times before, was another matter: it was carrying out the ritual, the symbolic act of aggression. Genet could steal only when a higher motive and risks were involved. If such motives were not operating, the unconscious forbade him to debase such an act, which had now taken on the aura of a religious experience. As Genet himself wrote later: "refusing to enumerate my exploits, I show what I owe them in the moral realm, what I build with them as a basis, what the simplest thieves are perhaps dimly seeking, what they themselves might achieve" (*TJ,* 94).

Genet's difficult pilgrimage into inferno and chaos had taken him back to France and to his prisons: the Santé, Tourelles, and Fresnes, among others. It was in prison, he told Sartre that he wrote his second poem:

> I was pushed into a cell where there were already several prisoners in "city" clothes. You're allowed to wear your jacket while you're still awaiting trial. But though I had filed an appeal, I was made, by mistake, to wear the

> prisoner's outfit. The weird get-up seemed to be a jinx. They despised me. I later had the greatest difficulty in overcoming their attitude. Among them was a prisoner who composed poems to his sister, idiotic, sniveling poems that they all admired. Finally, in irritation I said that I could do just as well. They challenged me and I wrote "The Condemned Man." I read it to them and they despised me even more. I finished reading it amidst insults and jeers. A prisoner said to me, "I write poems like that every morning." When I got out of jail, I made a particular point of finishing the poem which was all the more precious to me for having been despised.[8]

Genet had changed, slowly but incisively, physically as well as emotionally. From the soft, young, tender-eyed sixteen-year-old youth who had entered Mettray Reformatory, there had emerged the thirty-year-old hardened criminal. Or so he had thought—or wished—himself to be: "My face had hardened. The jaws are accentuated. The mouth is bitter and mean. I look like a hoodlum in spite of my eyes, which have remained gentle. Their gentleness is almost indiscernible because of the fixity of gaze imposed upon me by the official photographer" (*TJ*, 86). His Herculean labors, his descent into "sainthood," his negation of the state of man, these years of rigors he had forced himself to endure had brought him to a turn in the road. He had outgrown his chains. He had suffered. His pilgrimage was done. He had experienced desolation and solitude, every kind of humiliation and torture. He had permitted and longed for mankind to gouge out his liver while he bore the pain on the Promethean rock. His inner god, or divinity, had become manifest through his agony. The miracle had occurred. He was ready now to spew forth the experiences he had carved into his own soul: "it was within me that I established this divinity—origin and disposition of myself. I swallowed it. I dedicated to it songs of my own invention. At night I would whistle. The melody was a religious one. It was slow. Its rhythm was somewhat heavy. I thought I was thereby entering into communication with God: which is what happened. God being only the hope and fervor contained in my song. . . . Never would I have whistled to a light rhythm. I recognized the religious themes: they create Venus, Mercury, or the Virgin" (*TJ*, 86).

Genet was different from most other criminals. Indeed, he has been described as a "highly literate and memorable autodidact" with "an uncontrollable thirst for knowledge." He enjoyed reading and would seek out the prison libraries. Although small, they contained many of the classics: works of Pascal, Racine, Stendhal, and others that Genet read not once but many times. When not in prison, he sought out the Bibliothèque Nationale and other public libraries wherever he happened to be living at the time. The classics, of course, were always on his agenda, but so were works on metempsychosis, history, heraldry, architecture, mythology, and art. The ancient abbeys, cathedrals, and monasteries of France fascinated him, perhaps in part because many during the course of the centuries had been transformed into penal institutions. The information Genet gleaned from his readings was in time to be decanted into his writings.[9]

It was during the many dismal and lonely hours in prison that Genet began to write. From 1942 to 1949, he wrote first to last, poems, novels, plays, and a ballet. His words cascade forth, bursting, crackling out onto paper in glazed imagery. He brandished his words, always wearing the rictus or grin of pain, relieved every now and then by macabre humor.

For Genet the written word was alive—as if inhabited by a mysterious power, some hidden force that best conveyed his feelings, sensations, and ideas. The word was also capable of immortalizing the fleeting and transpersonalizing the individual event or personality involved in lyrical modes and a polyphonic language of signs. Via the word, language became discourse, and Genet was a master verbalist, drinking deeply of the word's essence, beauty, and sensuality, decanting its patterns onto paper in haunting images and rhythms.

The word enabled Genet to strip himself bare; it allowed the world to peer into a labyrinth, into a soul, but only on his terms, that is, through sham, deception, pretense, and pretext. "Writing brought me what I was looking for. . . . Not the anecdotes but the work of art. Not my life but its interpretation. That's what language offers me to evoke it, to speak of it, to translate it."[10]

Still, questions remain. Was Genet writing for himself? Was he trying to communicate his experiences to others? Was he returning to society? to life? Sartre wrote: "By infecting us with evil, Genet delivers himself from it. Each of his books is a cathartic attack of possession, a psychodrama; in appearance, each of them merely repeats the preceding one, as his new love affairs repeat the old; but with each work he masters increasingly the demon that possesses him. His ten years of literature are equivalent to a psychoanalytic cure."[11]

In 1947 Genet was in prison, serving out his tenth and last sentence. According to French law, one is sent up for life after ten violations. But Genet had already acquired a following in literary circles. Sartre, Cocteau, Mauriac, Gide, Mondor, and Claudel, among others, signed a petition appealing to French President Vincent Auriol to grant Genet a pardon. The presidential pardon was granted, and Genet was released from prison.

Since that time, he lived a free man. His writings brought him fame and money: *Our Lady of the Flowers, Miracle of the Rose, Funeral Rites, Quarrel of Brest, Deathwatch, The Maids, The Thief's Journal, The Balcony, The Blacks, The Screens,* and *A Captive in Love.* Genet traveled on the French Riviera, in Italy, North Africa, England, and wherever the spirit moved him. His homosexuality was part of his makeup. He had acquaintances, but still remained alone. The "tons of hatred" he once felt toward society, however, had almost disappeared: "You—that is, society—no longer interest me as an enemy. Ten or fifteen years ago I was against you. At the present time I'm neither for nor against you. We both exist at the same time, and my problem is no longer to oppose you, but to do something in which we're involved together, you and I alike" (*I*).

Genet owned nothing. He had no home. He stayed at the finest hotels sometimes, at the seamiest at others. He could live in total discomfort or in luxury; in cleanliness or in dirt, kempt or unkempt, depending upon his mood. Nor did either elegant or shoddy hotels alter his habits. If he needed a match to light his cigarette, for example, he did not hesitate to go "down into the dining room barefoot and in his pajamas" regardless of the class hotel. Nor did the idea of using the telephone to order something sent to his room occur to him. Genet usually ate little; particularly in later years, when he suffered from a kidney ailment and frequently had "only appetite . . . for alcohol and Nembutal." Nor did Genet use banks. If he happened to be in a large city and needed money he went to his publisher, Gallimard, or its representative, to ask for funds to be drawn on his royalties. If in a small town he went to the local book dealer who got in touch with the closest branch of Gallimard. Once he was given his money and put it in a little bag that he carried under his overcoat.[12]

Genet loved to talk about poetry, even reading his favorite verses aloud to friends. Although Baudelaire, Verlaine, and Rimbaud were perhaps his favorites, he virtually enshrined Mallarmé. When reading "Brise Marine," his high, thin voice quivered with feeling. After finishing, he paused and said: "Isn't it a miracle, that poem?" When asked whether the name Mallarmé meant anything in French, Genet "grinned" before answering: "His name indicates impotence: *mal-*

armé, n'est-ce pas? Poorly equipped sexually, but with a brain that made up for it."[13]

Genet was apolitical. "I hate all governments," he wrote. He did not attend government receptions, Cuban (although Castro was a friend of his) or otherwise. Only once did he sit at a table with a head of state—Georges Pompidou—because he had allowed certain of Genet's exiled companions to return to France.[14]

Genet was a loner who identified himself with the underdog: the black, the Arab, or the terrorist, as the case might be, but only insofar as they represented forces destined to overthrow existing regimes. He had no illusions as to the perfectibility of man, or as to one type of society being better than another. As Roger Blin said: "He does not try to substitute one order for another since he is against all order. . . . Genet offers no solution to problems, no new forms to replace old, no goals. This is because he feels that all order, all organizations are the beginning of new constraints."[15] Nor did Genet's last work, *A Captive in Love,* alter his stance. A captive by Genet's definition is not a prisoner but one in a position to blend and fuse—although only momentarily—with a nomadic community, with exiles and fighters.

Genet, however, admitted in *A Captive in Love,* "I am always sad." But at least, he added, he knew the reasons for his sadness.[16] He was preoccupied with both past and present, and silence, blackness, the void, dream, and death overshadowed his world—particularly in *A Captive in Love.* He wrote: "My life was thus composed of inconsequential gestures, inflated ever so subtly into audacious acts. Well, when I understood this, that my life was inscribed on emptiness, this emptiness was transformed into a terrible abyss" (*I*).

What then was Genet's answer? His *raison d'être?* His goal and direction, if any? We are told: "Toward oblivion. Most of our activities have the vagueness and vacantness of a tramp's existence. We very rarely make a conscious effort to transcend that state. I transcend it by writing" (*I*).

Genet was found dead in a hotel room on 15 April 1986: presumably he died as a result of throat cancer. He is buried in an abandoned Spanish Catholic cemetery at Larache, Morocco, about forty kilometers south of Asilah. A believer in no religion, Genet rests, ironically, alongside the French colonists (or *pieds-noirs*), for whom he felt such distaste. The small slab of white marble that marks his grave reads only, "Jean Genet, 1910–1986."

Chapter Two
Our Lady of the Flowers

> No doubt I shall be accused of common theft. I will not deny the accusation, I will simply retreat and not confront anyone who chooses to take the paltry word into his mouth. But the word—the poor, cheap, worn-out word, which does violence to all the finer meanings of life—is one thing and quite another the living primeval, and absolute deed, forever shining with newness and originality. It is only out of habit and sheer mental indolence that we come to regard them as the same thing. . . . Moreover, whenever it is a question of an act, it is not the what nor the why that matters . . . but simply the who. Whatever I have done and committed, it has always been first of all *my* deed. . . .
>
> —Thomas Mann, *Confessions of Felix Krull*

Notre-Dame-des-Fleurs (*Our Lady of the Flowers*) was written in 1942 while Genet was serving his sentence at Fresnes prison.[1] His novel was written on the brown paper that prison authorities gave convicts for the purpose of making bags. One day, when Genet had been taken from his cell to the Paris Law Court, he returned to find his manuscript gone. He was then called down to the warden's office and punished: three days in solitary confinement, and bread and water for using paper "that wasn't intended for literary masterpieces" (*I,* 46–47). Genet reacted to this treatment: "I felt belittled by the warden's robbery. I ordered some notebooks at the canteen, got into bed, pulled the covers over my head and tried to remember word for word, the fifty pages I had written. I think I succeeded" (*I,* 46–47).

Our Lady of the Flowers was written, Genet tells us, "sincerely, with fire and rage, and all the more freely because I was certain the book would never be read . . ." (*I,* 46–47). In this work Genet transposed and sublimated elements of his own life. His heroes, monsters, and saints are aspects of men he knew in prison, but mostly they are extensions of himself emerging like spectral shadows out of his fantasy.

The Narrative

The willed ambiguity of *Our Lady of the Flowers* is evident in the complexity of the novel's structure: the duality of time sequences as experienced by fictional and nonfictional protagonists and the concept of the sacred space implicit in both the images and the narrative sequences. Such labyrinthian and temporal/nontemporal qualities bring to mind Tzetan Todorov's statement concerning the distinctions between "The [temporality] of the universe represented and that of the discourse representing it."[2] Cyclic analepsis (flashbacks) and sequential duplicity in *Our Lady of the Flowers* serve to increase the conflicts between the characters themselves and between the reader and author in penetration of the text.[3] The world as revealed in *Our Lady of the Flowers* is perpetually mobile: the rational sphere is abolished, enabling the irrational and oneiric realm of signs and signals to surface, to yield to a new and enriched temporal reality. Indeed, Genet's "language of signs" or, to use Barthes' reference to "informational polyphony," serves to increase the complexity of both the novel's structure and of Genet's incredible intuitive faculties. Readers must work their way through this excitingly as well as repugnant, but ever-enriching experience that is Genet's creative world.[4]

The equivocal and complicated plot of *Our Lady of the Flowers* opens with a description of the narrator's heroes, Weidmann and Pilorge, killers guillotined young. The narrator has hung on the walls of his cell the newspaper photos of these and other criminals of a similar bent, thereby fusing his *temenos* (or sacred area) and the reader's diegetic or imagined space. The narrator sees something sacred in these "vacant-eyed heads" and frames the photos in stars made from colored glass beads, which prisoners are given for the purpose of decorating funeral wreaths (*OL,* 52). It is in honor of and with the aid of these heroes and lovers, both known and unknown to him, that the narrator tells us he wrote *Our Lady of the Flowers*.

Louis Culafroy, the son of Ernestine, one of the protagonists, was born in the country and comes to Paris as a young man of twenty. It is in this metropolis that he changes his name and also his way of life. Now known as Divine, he becomes a thief and male prostitute, and enjoys love affairs with Darling Daintyfoot, Our Lady of the Flowers, and others. Later, when Divine is older, he suffers because age has corroded his attractiveness. He is forced to support his lovers. "I'm a Valley of Desolation," he says. He dies of tuberculosis, a "Saint," in the narrator's words. Darling Daintyfoot, a male pimp who had been Divine's lover and who abandoned him after six years of life together, steals and is imprisoned for it. Our Lady of the Flowers, a sixteen-year-old, the youngest of the group, becomes Darling's and Divine's lover. He is the "perfect" hero, since he murders lucidly and fearlessly. He strangles a man of sixty-seven, confesses his crime to the police, and faces the guillotine as a superman, master of his emotions, stronger than death itself, since he is capable of annihilating fear.

"This book," Genet wrote, "aims to be only a fragment of my inner life" (*OL,* 52). Sartre called it "an epic of masturbation written at a time when Genet had regressed to a state of infantilism toward the childish narcissism of the onanist."[5] Living such a fantasy life was a way of escaping from the world, but it can also be considered as an attempt to find a deeper meaning in it. Genet, the passive dreamer, had become the active creator. He was now willing to grapple with words and matter in an endeavor to ground the fleeting figures that appeared before him through the veil of his dream state.

In *Our Lady of the Flowers* we come to know the sort of people Genet, as revealed through his characters, despised: the weak and the sentimental. Also presented are his ideal types: virile, ruthless, hard criminals who are unafraid of death. Genet dreamed of possessing his ideal men and built up a whole web of fantasy around them. He created a "cult of the murderer" and a "cult of the thief," upon which he *nourished* and *fed* himself. In this way he compensated for what he believed were his own deficiencies.

Not only are the strong set off against the weak in *Our Lady of the Flowers,* but young against old. The older men are ridiculed. The young men are forever making them suffer. The fact that Genet was growing older (he was thirty-two years old at the time he wrote this work) seems to have presented him with a serious emotional problem. He could not accept this natural occurrence gracefully and forever looked back upon his adolescence with nostalgia. He searched for the image of the adolescent he had once been in those he met, but was always destined to fail. He tried endlessly to recapture this period in his life, which he feared had slipped by him before it had ever been lived out: "I saw myself again in his face, especially in his forehead and eyes, and I was about to recognize myself completely when, bang, he smiled. It was no longer I, for in my childhood I could no more laugh, or even smile, than in any other period of my life. When the child laughed, I crumbled, so to speak, before my very eyes" (*OL,* 292).[6]

The Characters

Genet's characters have split personalities. One even says "Je suis *une* autre." They can never accept themselves or any part of their personality for what they are. Forever divesting themselves of their various characteristics, they wander aimlessly here and there, slipping in and out of situations. Such activities point to a rootlessness and instability within the character, the inability to dig inward, and the acceptance of merely scratching surfaces. Though they try to look inward, they are doomed to failure. So, events and relationships circumscribed in space and time are relatively unimportant for them. They are beyond the rational world. They live apart—in a realm of their own. What is of import to them, however, is the resonance set up within them by an external event.

The characters in *Our Lady of the Flowers* are not drawn in depth. They are like a series of silhouettes or facades moving across a stage. They are brittle and one-dimensional astral figures. Furthermore, they are at once male and female and are reminiscent of the figures of Minoan bullfighters and dancers depicted on ancient mural frescoes. The male figures in Cretan art were quite feminine in appearance, and the only way the artist in those days differentiated between the sexes was by his use of color.

The protagonists in this narrative are never tangible. They are always fleeting and are concerned only with the present, never with either past or future events. They are bound by no code, no morality, no ethics. There is no development of personality in the manner of Balzac or Stendhal, no heartrending episodes, no building up to climaxes. Genet's characters are detached, vacant shadows. They are reflections.

We learn that Divine is slim and lively, and that later on, when he is older, will become angular, much like Genet himself. He (she) who minces along, an aged and fallen drag queen, is also Louis Culafroy, a pained and troubled homosexual living in a drab neighborhood in Paris, amid hooligans and brutes.[8]

Divine's love for Darling will be "equivalent to despair"; he will, because of his sorrow, become the "great Fallen One" and "She who is soft." He tries to kill himself by taking poison so as to experience the "intolerable anguish," the effect of an unbelievable act and to admire the marvelous nature of an act so "madly irremediable." To take poison is another way of gaining victory over one's destiny, he believed, of surmounting death and thereby joining the select in the realm of the heroic. It is, in fact, suicide. But Divine is never strong enough to sever the bonds of life. He will wait for nature to cause his disintegration. Elsewhere, Divine is described as being made of "clear water" and will come to represent "astonishing tenderness," comparable to the noise a sandal makes when touching the stone of a temple's floor. Divine's eyes "sing despair" as he is carried along on "wings of fright."

Despite the fact that Divine is the butt of mockery even among homosexuals, and labeled an old whore, he seems to gather up enough strength to approach the absurdity of his situation. In a bar, on one occasion, when he suddenly begins to laugh, the crown he is wearing, consisting of a small tiara of false pearls, falls off and shatters on the ground. The pimps and fairies present are quick to mock his divestiture, humiliating him even more by uttering such statements as "The Divine is uncrowned!," whereupon his laughter becomes strident, drawing attention to himself once again, but intentionally. At this very moment, he removes his false teeth, places them on his head—the sign of a new crown—then spews forth: "Dammit all, Ladies, I'll be queen anyhow!" (*OL,* 181–82). All the epithets used by Genet to suggest Divine's character, which is fragile, tender, transparent, and yet very brittle and unbending, seem to be made of an amalgam of materials that lack physical depth and solidity.

Darling Daintyfoot, the pimp for whom Divine prostituted himself, loves to betray. He is hard and unfeeling and moves about only as his spirit dictates. He is described as being the "Eternal," the elegant, simple, smiling, handsome male, with hair like golden earrings. He is both "violent and tender, beatified . . . canonized." His torso rests on his hips, Genet wrote, "like a king on his throne." We learn further that there is something regal and awe-inspiring about Darling. Like Divine, however, he is unreal and one-dimensional. He is a silhouette stained against a sky, a half-being endowed with torso but no more, liquid and not solid.

Our Lady of the Flowers is also handsome and virile. His entrance into this drama is "solemn." He is imbued with a mystic feeling. He knows that he will be called upon, Genet writes, "to accomplish his destiny" and that his baptism has been a blood bath. Our Lady of the Flowers was born out of the narrator's love for Maurice Pilorge, the criminal who had been guillotined at the age of twenty for having killed his lover, Escudero, for a little money. The narrator was haunted by the image of Pilorge. He venerated this young man. He wanted to be like him and to kill as Pilorge had done in order to experience the ectasy of murder, the heroism, as Genet put it, of disdaining death: "To love a murderer. To love to commit a crime in cahoots with the young half-breed picture on the cover of the torn book. I want to sing murder, for I love murderers. To sing it plainly. Without pretending, for example, that I want to be redeemed through it, though I do yearn for redemption. I would like to kill" (*OL,* 120).

Ernestine, Divine's mother, represents the evil, grasping aspect of the mother archetype.[9] She is the mother who deserted Jean Genet at birth, the *son killer*. She is the "vagina dentata" who with "remarkable precision conceived "the whole mechanism of the drama" that is Divine's life. She is monstrous, vulgar, sensual, given to fits of rage, bitter, and has "brought forth a monstrous creature, neither male nor female . . ." (*OL,* 298) from her womb. She moves about in the book as a gesture, image, or presence and emerges as thinly drawn and as hollow as all the other characters.

There is one female figure who is drawn with warmth, Solange, a little girl whom Divine used to know where he lived in a hamlet with his mother. Solange is the antithesis of the evil mother, for Genet endowed her with ethereal qualities. As her name indicates, she is half sun (*sol*) and half angel (*ange*). She is deeply perceptive and has the ability of penetrating the impenetrable. But the feeling of tenderness and of understanding Divine experiences with her is doomed from the start. Solange is sent away to boarding school, and Divine leaves for Paris.

The realm depicted in *Our Lady of the Flowers* is inhabited by pimps, pederasts, and criminals. These beings are Genet's heroes and his gods. They are awe-inspiring and prowl about in mysterious ways. The young criminals, modeled upon Weidmann and Pilorge, are like stars come down to earth for him, "wounded aviators" piercing the inky clouds. Genet wished to be inhabited by their courage, strength, and virility. His admiration of their force was an admission on his part of his own weakness. Always wanting to be his heroes seeking communion with them both spiritually and sexually, he is distracted at this period in his life, from accepting his own image, smudged as it may have been.

Symbols

Like the symbolist poets, words for Genet are cloaked in mystery. They are hermetically sealed, and their meaning escapes slowly through association and analogy. To examine these symbols gives depth to what is otherwise one-dimensional.

It is in part by the medium of Genet's symbology that he imposes his colorful but hollow protagonists upon the reader. His creations are like empty shells or vases devoid of insides. They are never of flesh and blood, but move about like puppets gesticulating in a shadow theater. Their wills frequently become manifest through their gestures, silhouettes, gaits, and the rhythmic way in which they walk or dance. Their minutest motion, like the "infinitesimal movement of the finger of a Balinese dancer" ((*OL,* 283), is a symbol representing an otherwise indescribable sensation or thought. It is this world of symbols that must be penetrated for a clearer understanding of the motivations, inner turmoil, and preoccupations of Genet's characters. As he wrote in *Our Lady of the Flowers:* "a gesture is a poem and can be expressed only with the help of a symbol, always, always, the same" (*OL,* 156).

One of the most notable symbols is that of the prison and the cell: macrocosm and microcosm, a world within itself, a *temenos.* These circumscribed and womblike areas may be considered both destructive and positive, alienating and comforting. By limiting the convict's activities, he is forced to indwell, to meditate, to look within his own soul. Such activities, reminiscent of Plato's creatures as depicted in his "Allegory of the Cave" and of those initiates of the Eleusinian mysteries enchained in grottos within the earth, escaping only when seeing the "light," triggered the imagination as well as the psyche.[10] So, too, did Genet's beings live out their own secret mysteries, their rituals, in their own world: enclosed and restricted, evoking their handsome and virile Gods and heroes in newspaper cuttings, in photographs, framed with borders made of small glass beads that looked like wreaths, fashioned by the convict himself. These framed visualizations were prototypes of the "frame" of the book itself—and metaphors for the framed existences they were forced to lead in prison.

Another frequently used group of symbols in *Our Lady of the Flowers* is that of glass, windows, glaciers, ice, stars, diamonds. All these glass and glasslike substances and the shattering of them seem to indicate the characters' desire to look and smash the image they have of themselves. They seem to be unable to face what they see in a mirror, distorted as it may be, and they try desperately to find another image of themselves in the other mirrors and glasses with which Genet's book is replete. If new visualizations do not come forth, they will remain without an identity. The fright the protagonists experience in this domain is illustrated in the following description given by the narrator of windows looking out over a void: "I say vacant, for all the eyes are clear and must be sky-blue, like the razor's edge to which clings a star of transparent light, blue and vacant like the windows of buildings under construction, through which you can see the sky from the windows of the opposite wall" (*OL*, 52).

The void and the transparency here indicate the inner hollowness of the narrator's personality. The window, in this instance, acts as a barrier between himself and the image of himself he sees in it. The fact that the window stands empty against the sky signifies his desire to absorb the spiritual and reflective side of himself into the physical, and make of himself a blend or balance between the two. The image of the empty window also reveals the narrator's fear of death. Unless the void is filled, such an attitude, in psychological terms, implies a fear of death or decay of the soul. Divine also frequently experiences "a feeling of utter emptiness." He is lucid enough to know that he is merely living a shadowlike existence. He feels iced, therefore, when looking out on the empty coldness of the universe where there is no human warmth and no meaningful relationship.

Frequently, therefore, Genet's characters are perched high above the rest of humanity: on balconies and stairways. Divine, who wants to amuse himself one day, loosens the latticework from a balcony in order to lure a two-year-old child to its death. The child's death, symbolically speaking, is a premonition of Divine's fall or death, that is, the death of the child within him. The use of the negative imagery of falling down into a void indicates Divine's fear of being annihilated, not only by his own instinctuality, but by society and all those who surround him.

There are, however, positive aspects to the image of the balcony: It looks out beyond the world below, and if a balance is kept between the spiritual and the physical sides of man, between alienation from reality and submersion within it, the person standing on that balcony can embrace the world and be nourished by it. In this connection, the symbol of the balcony grows in importance as Genet's writing evolves.

Stairs, as a symbol, lead upward to heaven or to "Logos," the spirit within man. It is these stairs that Genet's heroes always seem to be endlessly climbing, trying as hard as they can to encourage their spiritual half to impose itself or at least to counterbalance their instinctual impulses. But their endeavors seem futile and, like the story of the Tower of Babel, end in confusion.

As there is, in Genet's work, a symbolic conflict between heights and depths, so there is one between colors. Red fire images, for example, with their scorching and destructive aspects, also have their positive side in Genet's symbology. They serve to light the path leading out of his character's maze of emotions. Flaming-cloud images, therefore, are usually contrasted by him with black, symbolizing confusion, degradation, and death. In the following illustration, such antithesis is used to denote character. Montmartre is "blazing" as Divine crosses the street with its "multi-colored lights" and enters into the "night." To describe the warring sentiments experienced in love, a brilliant black is employed: "You are a sun brought into my night. My night is a sun brought into yours!" This last image indicates the character's longing for inner harmony, for a merging of opposites.

The frequent juxtaposition of the aforementioned jarring colors are a verbal indication of the author's enormous psychic energy. Indeed, the intensity of the somber tones used in *Our Lady of the Flowers* is frequently measured by the brilliance of the contrasting red and black images and the emotions they evoke: "O Pilorge! Your face, like a lone nocturnal garden in Worlds where Suns spin round! And on it that impalpable sadness, like the light trees in the garden. Your face is dark, as if in broad daylight a shadow had passed over your soul" (*OL*, 120).

Flowers play an important role in Genet's symbology. Many of Genet's criminals are endowed with flowered names: Our Lady of the Flowers, Mimosa I, II, IV. Our Lady of the Flowers is described as having the physical and moral character of a flower in the vegetal, germinative sense. By this same token, Divine feels more virile in his presence. Flowers are also used to describe various gestures and aspects of a character. When Divine walks, he throws rose, rhododendron, and peony petals all about him. There is a strange affinity between Genet's characters and flowers. The flower is a symbol of the self, of purity, of the Virgin Mary. The golden flower and the blue flower represent, according to the medieval alchemists, the hermaphrodite.[11] Such a symbol is another indication of the character's desire to experience a union of opposites, or inner harmony and wholeness.

There is still another reason for Genet's attraction for flowers. Young flowerlike gods were worshiped in antiquity. They were always doomed to die young because they were unable to break the bonds that constricted their progression. They were, therefore, symbolically speaking, very close to the state of the sacrificed child. Hyacinth, for example, was one of these divine boys. He was loved by Apollo. One day while Apollo and he were hurling the discus, the god struck "his beloved" with the stone slab and killed him. From Hyacinth's blood arose the flower with his name. It is claimed that the bulb of this flower could be effectual in postponing a boy's puberty. It is also said that pederasty started with Hyacinth. Narcissus, another "flower god," fell in love with his own image when he was sixteen years old and, as a result, pined away.[12] Genet, like Hyacinth and Narcissus, was a sacrificed child, an adolescent who had never succeeded in passing beyond the homosexual phase of his emotional development.

For Genet, the flower also symbolizes the criminal. The flower, in this connection, is a beautiful and heroic plant that accepts its ephemeral nature. The criminal too, according to the narrator of *Our Lady of the Flowers,* accepts courageously the consequences of his actions and the vicissitudes of his brief life. The flower, like the criminal, is dual: spiritual, in that it looks up toward the heavens, and physical, because it is rooted in the earth. Derrida writes the following concerning the flower: "the Flower, which signifies (symbolizes, metaphorizes, metonymizes, and so on) the phallus, once caught in the syntax of the cuttable-culpable, signifies death, decapitation, decollation? Anthologies signifying the signifier signifying castration?"[13]

Genet's Canvas: His Impressionistic Style

Genet constructs his novels through a series of impressions in the manner of Monet or Proust. Descriptions of domiciles and landscapes fade into one another, are superimposed upon one another, merge and converge.

Divine's funeral scene, for example, illustrates Genet's impressionism. This scene begins with a description of Divine's room, which represents the land of the living. Divine's window, however, looks out upon the Montmartre cemetery, which symbolizes the other aspect of himself—the unrevealed, destructive part, which eventually leads to the deterioration of his body and soul. Both worlds are described almost simultaneously. Before learning much more about Divine, the reader witnesses his funeral. A funeral cortege, chanting somberly, then merges with a crowd swaying in sadness. It is here that Genet entices his readers more boldly to follow him into his image by appealing to their senses of touch, sight, and smell: "In the rain, this black cortege, bespangled with multi-colored faces and blended with the scent of flowers and rouge, followed the hearse. The flat round umbrellas, undulating above the ambulating procession, held it suspended between heaven and earth" (*OL,* 67). The atmosphere is heavy and dank with rain. One examines the picture more closely and sees a priest singing the *dies irae.* The priest walks forward in the mud as if he were in a forest, a foreign land. The mystery of the funeral cortege gives Genet the opportunity of introducing another impression, of extending his dream fantasy and seeing this same priest in another light, as a young man with a splendid body, dancing and stepping lightly and rhythmically. Suddenly, Genet's sentences accelerate, as though marking time to a fast beat. Then the dream vanishes. The funeral proceeds; the body is lowered into the ground to the sound of Psalm singing. Divine's saga is over. Yet, it is not over; he will appear in another series of impressionistic images.

Genet's descriptions are like tapestries, woven with brilliant strands and left untarnished by time. His colors, depending upon his mood, became vibrant and harsh and at other moments delicate and feminine, embedded usually in luxurious magnificence. The following passage from *Our Lady of the Flowers,* with its cutting and breaking of colors, its crashing of image upon image, is a composite of tender, almost effeminate colors and images, and of brutal ones expressing both facets of his character's chaotic nature: "She had fired in the apartment with the garnet-red velvet, and the bullet shattering the beveled mirrors, the pendants, the crystals, the stucco, the stars tearing the hangings—in short, destroying the structure which collapsed brought down not sparkling powder and blood, but the crystal of the chandelier and the pendants . . ." (*OL,* 66).

It would seem that Genet had a need to people his universe with satins, silks, and delicate fabrics, as well as with knives and guns. Divine's fingers, for example, are of a delicate nature, like lace; his bed is always "hidden in lace" and surrounded by a "universe of lace." Divine's mother, Ernestine, on the other hand, has a brutal personality in complete accordance with Genet's descriptions of her: "so Ernestine agreed to kill only on condition that she avoid the horror that the here below would not fail to inspire her (convulsions, squirting blood and brain, reproaches in the child's dismayed eyes) and the horror of an angelic beyond . . ." (*OL,* 64).

Genet's descriptions are, at times, overly saturated with objects. But it is through his skillfully combined overabundance of things that he satirizes society's materialism. Ernestine's room, for example, is drenched in rococo, and Divine's is bathed in color, filled with bric-a-brac and all sorts of disparate objects *à la* Cocteau of the *Terrible*

Children: "the room descended till it blended with a luxurious apartment, odorned with gold, the walls hung with garnet-red velvet, the furniture heavy but toned down with red faille curtains. . . . The floor was covered with thick blue and violet carpets" (*OL,* 64). The velvets, thick carpeting, chandeliers, and heavy furniture are all things and possessions that crush and overwhelm man, that stifle and make him a prisoner of matter. To be a slave of objects is to be a slave of society and its counterpart, "the great mother."

Juxtaposed to sumptuous decors are ugly ones, which become an aesthetic equivalent of Genet's own ambivalent attitude toward possessions: his aesthetic love for beautiful things and his distaste for man's dependency upon them: "That evening she was wearing a champagne silk short-sleeved blouse, a pair of blue trousers stolen from a sailor, and leather sandals. On one of her fingers though preferably on the pinkie, an ulcer-like stone gangrened her" (*OL,* 71).

The images, colors, and perfumes that emanate from Genet's prose will be caught up in strange rhythms to fit the occasion and the emotion expressed. The sentences will swell and deflate, accelerate and slacken in pace, in order to capture and hold the reader's attention. "Divine's saga should be mimed," Genet wrote, and indeed, Darling, his friend, is once portrayed as dancing "the java" with his hands in his pockets. Divine swirls and swishes in his room and looks like a darting jelly fish as he falls in with the wind that fluffs up the grass about and between the swaying cypress trees around the cemetery. He is in rhythm with the exterior world and the "spectral agitation of the dead."

It is through Genet's stylistic techniques—his impressionism, his use of color, the juxtaposition and antithesis of his images, and the rhythms and counterrhythms of his prose—that he reveals, in part, the beings he projects from his unconscious world. But who are these shadow personalities who compel the narrator to ask himself, "What monsters continue their lives in my depths?" (*OL,* 22).

The Sacred and Divine Drama

We discover in *Our Lady of the Flowers* that each of the characters, in his own fashion, is involved in a profound search—for his soul and for God. In fact, each being is flooded with God. Nature, in which God dwells, is, therefore, sacred. The cosmos, an emanation of God, is part of a divine drama and feast, and as such is alive and vibrant. To penetrate into nature's world or God's world is to dig through the integuments of matter that conceal it and to discover the realm of primordial unity and, thereby, one's own roots and sources. To enter into the divine realm is to undergo a religious experience. The protagonists in *Our Lady of the Flowers* live their religious experiences and carry out their rituals as they understand them—in a primitive manner suited to their primitive souls.

To sanctify his creatures, which is Genet's intent, is to purify them through pain and anguish. About Divine, he writes: "Slowly but surely I want to strip her of every vestige of happiness so as to make a saint of her" (*OL*, 98). She is transformed spiritually by her poverty, suffering, and multiple humiliations at the hands of her lover, Darling, who finally abandons the passive and aging homosexual. The body language, however, reveals an inner deterioration: with arched body, his head hanging down, the reader observes Divine's murmurings—"Lord, I am among Thy elect"—with gestures worthy of a theatrical performance.

A preoccupation with God is manifest from beginning to end of *Our Lady of the Flowers*. This narrative, which unfolds on several levels—in prison, in the country, in Paris, in various dives, and in deserted and crowded streets with their eerie phantoms and criss-crossing shadows—is more or less enclosed in the gigantic image of a cathedral or monastery. Indeed, the characters come forth, like cackling and grimacing gargoyles perched outside a cathedral, and enter their own private houses of worship. The prison cell is symbolically transformed into a cathedral with all of its mysteries and miracles, both sexual and spiritual, taking place before the reader's eyes, its litanies being chanted by the inmates, its confessions being heard.

Because Genet was forever converting French abbeys and cathedrals built in both the medieval times and during the *ancien régime* into prisons, he was in effect creating a "feudalistic hierarchy" for the reader. Within its sacred walls there existed a courtly culture and important knightly relationships: the older warriors were served by pages; priests, by acolytes; tyrants, "by those who suited their fancies."[14]

Prison objects are similarly metamorphosed: the simple prison bed upon which a convict lies turns into an altar; Divine wants to "say Mass on Darling's chest"; the law court where Our Lady of the Flowers reveals his crime becomes a confession booth; communion is taken in Divine's room amid resplendent jewels, either fake or real; soft, colorful, frilly cloths, and white enamel lilies. Billowing forth from each character, object, and area are the incense, the benumbing odors, those pungent and suffocating human smells that always accompany a Genet hero and contribute to the mystery of the scene. The pictures of murderers framed in colored glass that are placed on the walls of the cold bleak cell turn into stained-glass windows stamped with glazed images of Our Lady of the Flowers, Divine, First Communion, and other characters.

Though Genet lives and breathes God, and this is obvious throughout *Our Lady of the Flowers* as has already been mentioned, he rejects organized religion. He goes still further. He satirizes it on every possible occasion. First, the names he chooses for his protagonists, Our Lady of the Flowers, Divine, First Communion, Archangel Gabriel, revealed Genet's preoccupation with God, but not the god that *man* created in *his* own image. Second, instead of finding the religious types one would expect with characters bearing such hallowed names, Genet's protagonists turn out to be "pimps," "queens," "faggots," "aunties." Genet makes a mockery of organized religion, but *never* of God, only man's limited interpretation of him.

Everything is an emanation of the divine, and worship in any form serves divinity.[15] Genet's heroes are all infused with divine will. They are not ashamed or frightened of their actions before God (or gods) because they knew they are carrying out his will on earth in all of their rituals. Worship in any form serves divinity. Access to the divine realm, that *other world* with which they long to merge, requires enormous energy on their part. This energy can and is expressed both spiritually and sexually.

Divine, therefore, serves God as he sees fit. In Divine, we find the androgyne, the monist's *one,* for he is at once man and woman and shifts easily from one sex to the other. His clothes are both masculine and feminine and so are his strident screams and husky laughter. His room is his "Vatican," and he is its "supreme pontiff." Darling and Divine go to Mass at the Madeleine carrying a "gold-clasped" missal.

Divine's love never causes him to fear God's anger, Jesus' disdain, or the Virgin's disgust. On the contrary, he makes of his love a God above God, Jesus, and the Holy Virgin. He accepts the life his God has cut out for him, for it will lead him to Him. In other terms, he has surrendered his *will* to God and consequently does not and cannot exercise an objective *will.* All the homosexuals depicted by Genet have given up or renounced their *wills.* They are merely carrying out the *will* of God, who lives within them. Meister Eckhart, the mystic, believed that when man gives up his will to the care of the prelate, he has no will of his own, and so God must will for him. If God were to neglect him,

He would be neglecting Himself. Therefore, God commands for man what He would command for Himself.

Since Genet's heroes are carrying out God's will, part of God dwells within them, and they are, in part, God. Divine, therefore, is part God and can transform himself at will (God's will) into a chimera[16] or a griffin[17]—both monstrous and awe-inspiring beasts—or into a clucking hen or a nymph. Darling turns into Andromeda's sea monster. Divine and Darling are at times theriomorphic divinities who partake in Egyptian and Grecian mysteries; at other moments they have human faces or are made of matter. But whatever they are, it is always God who is acting, not they. God chooses a thousand different ways in which to enter man's body: as a shower of gold,[18] a swan,[19] a bull,[20] a dove,[21] and so forth.

Genet's cosmogony is peopled with angels and archangels, those purely spiritual beings created by God to manifest his will on earth. Divine calls a soldier whom he loves Archangel Gabriel,[22] and whenever "Prince-Monseigneur," as the two are called, walk down the street, people seem to sense divinity within this couple and bless them. Divine takes on the stature of a biblical angel and can rise like a "column of smoke." In this fashion, he becomes carbonized before God's throne and is changed into a vaporous, translucid being—God's messenger.

God within each being *acts*. Darling was predestined at birth, Genet wrote, during a "brief but mysterious baptismal ceremony" at which angels and Divinity were present, to go to limbo after death. Because of this augury, Darling's life is "golden" and "enveloped in a lukewarm and feeble halo. . . ." Divine and Darling both go to Mass and walk without seeing; they shiver when taking communion as they introduce the host into themselves.

Our Lady of the Flowers is another being through whom God's will becomes manifest. Our Lady of the Flowers is the sublime murderer. He will "confess" his crime to Darling, as though he were telling it to his priest in one of the cubicles in the Madeleine church, and then at court to judge and jury. The audience at court is electrified and shivers "like taffeta" and it listens to Our Lady of the Flowers' revelation. Our Lady of the Flowers stands like Christ, we are told, erect and strong, inspired by the strength divinity has infused in him at this moment. When the verdict of death is handed down, it is like an "apotheosis." The guards treat Our Lady of the Flowers with "awe" because he seems to have something "sacred" about him. They know he is "charged with the sins of the world" and act as though they want to be blessed and redeemed by him. Forty days later, at the dawn of a spring day, Our Lady of the Flowers' head is sheared off by the guillotine. "He flew away." He is "carried away by Angels."

The immensity of space and time frightened Genet's characters as it had Pascal three centuries earlier. Like Pascal too, the creatures peopling *Our Lady of the Flowers* understood loneliness and solitude. Unlike Pascal, they did not wear a hair shirt or flagellate themselves in order to be worthy of heaven in the afterlife. They tortured themselves, however, emotionally, by imposing suffering of all sorts upon themselves and those they loved. Yet they indulged the flesh to the utmost; they tasted all there was to taste in this domain, and it is through this communion with the living, through the "phallus" as a symbol of man's creative energy, that each sought God's domain.

That the phallus should play the enormous role it does in Genet's work is not astounding, since it is one of the most powerful natural symbols known to man. It is around the worship of the phallus as a source of creative energy that Genet's philosophy will be centered. Divinity can be reached both through spirituality and sexuality. For Genet, they are one.

It must be recalled that religious rituals since the dawn of mankind have been bathed in sexual imagery. St. Augustine, for example, in his *Sermo suppositus* wrote: "Like a bridegroom Christ went forth from his chamber, he went out with a presage of his nuptials into a field of the world. He came to the marriage-bed of the cross, and there, in mounting it, he consummated his marriage. And when he perceived the sighs of the creature, lovingly gave himself up in place of his bride, and he joined himself to the woman (matrona) for ever."[23]

One need merely open Sir James George Frazer's *The Golden Bough* to understand how closely the sexual act, whether symbolic or actual, is part and parcel of religion. For example, the Zapotec priests in southern Mexico, especially the high pontiff, would, on certain days, become drunk, and while in this state take the most beautiful of the virgins consecrated to the service of the gods. If she gave birth to a son, he was brought up as a prince. Sexual rites were practiced particularly at seasonal festivals. Among certain African tribes, sexual intercourse was required at calendar crises relating to vegetation and also as a means of reinvigorating the community in times of trouble. Rolling, considered a similar custom, occurs in May before the reaping of flax in Portugal. Nuptial unions between mortals and immortals were held to be practiced in Greece: one recalls the tales of Europa, Alcmena, Danae, and others. The rituals of mystery religions in both Greece and Rome included many sexual practices. Men and gods were one. Many Roman kings, for example, claimed to be the representative or embodiment of Jupiter. Many families traced their descent from divinity. Prostitution in some cases was considered sacred. Saint Mary of Egypt prostituted her way to Jerusalem. Virgins gave themselves to holy men and became the brides of God. They mated ritually with the kings or priests, who impersonated a god in such ceremonies as the "sacred marriage."[24]

Many primitive peoples felt that to commune with God meant "sexual union." during which time man was taking in the "innermost essence and power of a god, his semen."[25] Therefore, a purely sensual idea became a "sacred act," especially when "a god is represented by a human deputy or by his symbol, the phallus." In initiation ceremonies in New Guinea, for example, the initiate could only eat food mixed with sperm and was given the care of a newborn. The body and everything pertaining to it was sanctified.[26] The spiritual experience was so intense that any emanation from deity was totally accepted and acceptable.

The sexual act is an externalization of inner processes. The phallus considered symbolically is the most powerful manifestation of man's inner energy. In Greece, for example, the worshipers of Dionysus, the Maenads, or Bacchantes reached such a peak of ecstasy during the religious worship that they reveled in all sorts of erotic orgies. They wore long robes, their heads thrust back were wreathed in ivy, and they carried a *thyrsus* (a phallic symbol: a long staff with a pine cone on its end). Pentheus wanted to stop the Bacchanalian orgies and the worship of the phallus. Dionysus rendered him mad for such sacrilege. As a result, he donned women's clothing and himself joined in the ravings. In a state of insane ecstasy, his mother mistook him for a lion that was sacred to Dionysus and tore him to pieces. Such was the punishment meted out to one who had contempt for this aspect of man: his instinctuality.

It is through the phallus that Genet's characters reach divinity. Perhaps their search for divinity is their way of expressing their need for love through contact with the divine. Human love is considered at times to be a necessary step leading to the divine presence. According to the Gospel of John, "God is love, and he who abides in love abides in God, and God abides in him." Love manifests itself at some moments as *concupiscentia* and in other instances as "spiritual affection." Genet's heroes in *Our Lady of the Flowers,* who experiences a bodily union throughout the novel and at times whose life revolves around bodily union, greet God in both manners: instinctually and spiritually, since they are *one* for them.[27]

Writers such as Cocteau and Valéry considered *Our Lady of the Flowers* one of Genet's finest works. Some American critics, such as Lionel Abel, looked upon it as "the greatest novel . . . since Faulkner."[28]

In *Our Lady of the Flowers,* Genet's creatures, whose hollow and rootless personalities are revealed not only through their actions and desires, but through vocabulary as well, reflect in a sense the author's own literary state. Still groping as a writer, creating intuitively although rashly, not fully aware of the direction his literary endeavors would take, Genet is still a long way from the detached artist/creator of *The Screens,* who manipulates his marionettes with ease and dexterity.

Chapter Three

The Miracle of the Rose

> I know the heavens bursting with lightning, and the whirl-
> winds
> And the undertow and the currents: I know night,
> Dawn passionate like a flock of doves,
> And I have seen sometimes, what man believes he has
> seen!
>
> (Arthur Rimbaud, *The Drunken Ship*)

Miracle de la Rose (The *Miracle of the Rose*) was written in La Santé Penitentiary in Paris in 1943 where Genet had been imprisoned for theft. It is an autobiographical novel and is based on Genet's experiences in the prisons of Fontevrault, where hardened criminals were sent, and Mettray, a reformatory.

As a lad Genet had been unable to face the isolation of his life. He compensated for the lack of affection or genuine warmth in real life by contriving a world of fantasy and living in it. There was no solicitous mother to tell him the stories of "Jack and the Bean Stalk" or "The Sword in the Stone." He had to invent them himself. His universe, a prison, was transformed by the wizardry of his imagination not only into a monastery, but into a castle filled with luxurious ornaments and nobles and gentlemen of the court. In the *Miracle of the Rose* Genet recreates for the reader his magic world, one of dazzling beauty, charged with novelty and excitement. Rarely did Genet see reality for what it was. Rather, he saw into things and beings and created a world to suit his fancy. He poetized reality, just as Merlin had whipped up his magic brew.

In like manner, Genet created a "cult of the criminal," which he describes in the *Miracle of the Rose.* He looked upon his robberies, he tells us, symbolically, as heroic and religious acts. He felt a mysterious veneration for the implements he used while performing the rituals of thievery, two wedges and a crowbar. He was hypnotized by his tools and slept near them as a warrior rests near his armaments or a monk near his relics and crosses. He was possessed by the click of the lock when he opened the door of the first apartment he robbed at Auteuil, by the silence and feeling of solitude that followed, and the mystery of the objects that surrounded him. All these objects, implements, and occurrences that preceded the act of robbery were vehicles by which Genet entered into a new dimension. In this *other* realm of mysteries and essences, platonic in a sense, he became, in his imagination, a young sovereign or god.

When in prison, Genet's lack of emotional self-sufficiency was apparent in all of his love affairs that are related in the *Miracle of the Rose.* His relationships became magnified and were not looked upon in a realistic manner, but rather in a surrealistic one. Genet felt elevated and purified, he writes, by the experiences he had lived through with his lovers and the emotions they had engendered. These lover-convicts became a singular manifestation of an immense love that Genet wanted to share with others.

On the other hand, Genet felt humiliated when deserted by Bulkaen, whom he courts, thus remaining only the mistress of Divers, another of the prison's Macho figures. Interestingly, Genet applies, certainly unconsciously, society's sex-gender views to the world of the homosexual. As a queen, he sees himself playing the feminine role: weak and inferior to the male who is superior to her since he is purported to be tough and strong. Nevertheless, Genet still holds the trump card because he realizes that intelligence and moral courage—attributes that are his—are superior to mere physical power.

What sets the *Miracle of the Rose* apart from Genet's other works and makes it unique among them is the profound mystical experience he underwent in Fontevrault prison and the intensity with which he recounts it in narrative. The author's visionary experience, or the "miracle," as he called it in this novel, put him face to face with deity, the transcendental being within him—the self. Such a *revelation* shook him profoundly, and, as a result, it influenced the direction his whole life was to take from then on. He learned from this *miracle* that his path lay not in an *outward* search, but rather in an *inward* one.

A stylistic change is also discernible in the *Miracle of the Rose.* The impressionistic style used in *Our Lady of the Flowers* is less obvious in this narrative. It is now used mainly as a means of merging past with present, Mettray with Fontevrault, thereby obliterating the rational conception of time and space. Genet employs realism, to some extent in the *Miracle of the Rose,* as a stylistic technique to add to the credibility of his narrative. Such a change in emphasis indicates, to a certain degree, the author's willingness to communicate with society, to emerge from the dream visions that had previously held him captive.

In the *Miracle of the Rose* we are introduced in detail to the prisons of Fontevrault, formerly a monastery, and Mettray, a reformatory. The disciplines, the prisoners' dress, and the living conditions are described with passion and realism. The reader also learns of the emotional attachments and anguishes experienced by the narrator in his love relationships with Bulkaen, Harcamone, and other inmates and the close affinity that he felt existed between prison and religion. Lengthier recounting of events is unwarranted, since the bulk of the book deals with the narrator's sexual experiences with his fellow inmates.

Prison and Religion

That there should be an alliance between prison and religion may at first seem strange, but not so when one realizes that many prisons in France were once monasteries, abbeys, or retreats. Fontevrault had been a Benedictine abbey. The narrator's mystic experiences at Fontevrault were rooted in reality: a house of religion transformed into a prison.

Fontevrault is situated sixteen miles from Saumur. It was founded as an abbey in 1099 by Robert d'Arbrissel, who instituted a new type of regulation. Religious orders were usually headed by an abbot. Fontevrault, however, was different in that it included separate convents for men and women, the latter headed by an abbess. It was in this abbey that Henry II, a Plantagenet (Genet points to the affinity of names between Planta*genet* and his own), his wife, Eleanor of Aquitaine, Richard the Lion-Hearted, and Elisabeth, the wife of Jean Sans Terre, were buried. Fontevrault's Benedictine order was suppressed in 1790, and the buildings were converted into a house of detention.

The present prison inmates of Fontevrault, according to the narrator, carry out the traditions of the nuns and monks who once inhabited the abbey. Like the monks who used to serve the Lord, the convicts today pray, lament, and work in silence, either in wood, stained glass, or stone-cutting; they wear rough, dark clothes and perform mystical and religious rites: "The prison lived like a cathedral at midnight on Christmas. We were carrying on the tradition of the monks, who went about their business at night in silence. We belonged to the Middle Ages."[1] The "indescribable" religious ceremonies carried on around the tombs of the Plantagenets and Richard the Lion-Hearted by the monks, abbesses, or nuns, have been forgotten by most, but not, however, by the convicts incarcerated at Fontevrault. They are, even now, continuing according to their own fashion and understanding, an inverted version of the strange, secret rituals in those windowless regions of the prison.

As in a monastery, prison, or "colony," discipline both at Mettray and Fontevrault is severe: rising at six; dressing, washing, breakfasting; working at the shop until six; to the dormitories at seven. The prison was made up of ten separate houses. The inhabitants of each house were considered by the inmates as belonging to a family. Each family was given a letter for a name—*A, B, C, D, E, F, G, H, J, L*—and was composed of thirty "children." Sometimes names were given unofficially by the prisoners and guards to a family, "The Family of Joan of Arc," for example.

Genet was fascinated by the image of Joan of Arc. This mythical figure was, to be sure, saintliness personified since she fought, was imprisoned, and died a martyr for her country. Genet, however, associates her with other attributes: since she wore men's clothing, he saw her as a transvestite. The figure of Marie Antoinette also mesmerized Genet: she had been accused of incest, theft, and lesbianism, and had been imprisoned and beheaded like the heroes of crime he so admired.[2]

Genet and his fellow prisoners created a whole secret hierarchy within each family cell. The strongest and most vicious member of the family was appointed "older brother" by the head of the family, who was then served by a young boy called a page, confidant, or lady-in-waiting.

When the narrator was sixteen, Mettray was his universe and *B* his family. The cells were the rooms of his home and the convicts his relatives. It was at Mettray, about which he writes with nostalgia, that he alleviated his loneliness with his "family," his lovers. The love he found in his homosexual relationships with Divers and Bulkaen was like an "enchanted" brew, different from the one Tristan and Isolde imbibed, but just as basic and meaningful to him.

The prison, the narrator's earthly dwelling place, became for him what the monasteries of old had been for monks. It was in this environment that he found a family and served God. The narrator was infused with God's spirit, he wrote, after sexual union with his lovers. Such divine spirit as entered him during these moments gave him strength to continue his labor of living.

The prison-religion atmosphere encouraged the narrator's fantasies to such an extent that an inner transformation became discernible in his psyche.[3] To begin to understand how and why this inner transformation occurred, one must examine the imagery and the symbolism used in the *Miracle of the Rose.*

Imagery and Symbolism

The narrator was "cultivating darkness," he wrote, that is, he was plunging into his own unconscious in order to find light. He saw everything as symbolic. Animals, plants, people, buildings, and cells were all weighed with meaning; the sky was "abstract," obscure, and dangerous. Each image and symbol had its own private reservoir of meanings and sensations.

When the narrator arrived at Fontevrault for the first time, he was moved by the "mysterious power" of his penitentiary, its "aura" and "magic." He felt as though he had reached the bottom of a valley in the center of which stood a miraculous fountain.

The fountain symbol here indicates that an inner unconscious transformation was about to occur. The image of the fountain implies a "bringing up" from mother earth or from the unconscious of certain energy or life-giving substances. Such intense psychic activity as the narrator was now experiencing unconsciously and as revealed by the fountain image could make for growth if the psychic energy were properly assimilated by the conscious mind. It could, however, lead to death if the conscious mind were overpowered by the forces of the unconscious. Water can both quench and drown. In the narrator's case, the struggle was still on. No solution was yet in sight.[4]

While at Fontevrault the narrator dreamed he was standing on the peak of a rock. He enjoyed this position because of the altitude that isolated him and put him above others. The narrator's ambivalent feelings toward people were expressed by the rock's height. He was *high* and removed from the world. He hated society, which he felt might stifle and submerge him. Yet he was forever torn by his desire to belong to some kind of society, in prison or elsewhere. The narrator wanted to be a loner, yet he suffered acutely from loneliness.

In addition, the narrator tells us that he was obsessed by the blue eagle his lover Bulkaen had tatooed on his chest.[5] When the narrator looked at the eagle as well as at Bulkaen's blond hair, green eyes, and supple body, he was seized with "sacred dread." The narrator had become double. Up there, flying with Bulkaen's eagle, as if in a mirror of blue, he could look down upon his other wordly self, his enchained half, and grimace. Such alienation from reality had swept over Julien

Sorel, hero of Stendhal's *The Red and the Black,* when he stood on a mountain top watching a bird of prey and the scenery about him, in a world he would someday conquer, he thought. The eagle had been Napoleon's symbol, that of the strong man. Bulkaen was the same strong-man type, audacious and arrogant, the bird-of-prey personality the narrator would like to have been.

Genet projected onto Bulkaen, as he had upon his other fictional lovers, those characteristics he lacked, and in so doing activated the deepest layers of his unconscious. The strength, the bravura he adored in his heroes, and with which he endowed them in general, was a coverup for his own shaky self. Genet at Mettray was like an edifice built on air, a skyscraper constructed on quicksand—grasping everywhere at anything to maintain some semblance of balance.

The Ship Image

The image of the ship appears so frequently in the dreams recounted in the *Miracle of the Rose* that it must be considered separately. It is the ship as a symbol that permits the narrator, and Genet by extension, to penetrate into another realm and so escape the confines of the closed prison atmosphere as well as those of the rational mind. With Genet, as he appears in his work the *Miracle of the Rose,* as with Rimbaud, the author of the poem "The Drunken Ship," the ship represents not only a way of escape, but also of discovery, the breaking away from reality and the unearthing of a deeper world.

Strange things occurred to the narrator in his dream state. For example, he saw himself in a boat. The air about him in those watery mists, he tells us, was transformed into a series of fiery sparks, indicating the volcanic brutality and charged atmosphere of the dreamer's emotions. Such sparks and mists as he saw in his dream made it almost like a creation scene. Things were still obscure with him, but something was going on, fermenting and bursting with life: "The air was sparkling. My pane is frosted over, and it is indeed a joy to see the frost. . . . The air is sparkling. Mettray suddenly takes the place—not of the prison in which I live—by of myself, and I embark, as formerly deep in my hammock, on the remains of the half-destroyed unmasted ship among the flowers of the Big Square at Mettray. My longing for flight and love disguises her as a mutinous galley that has escaped from a penal colony" (*M,* 89).

On one dream excursion on a ship, the narrator, the nightly wanderer, found himself face to face with stars on open water. He began studying the significance of the stars, and they seemed to reflect his soul state. He tried to reach up to them spiritually, and he felt an affinity with all of their power and brilliance. The higher he went, the greater was his immersion in the cosmos, its heights and depths. Such a dream implied that the narrator placed himself in the center of these radiant forces, that he had found an orientation, and that he was related to his surroundings.

On occasion, the ship would emerge solitarily on an expanse of sea. The narrator would see a face, a body, usually that of a young man, on the boat. In one dream there was a captain. Together, he and the captain experienced ecstatic spiritual and sexual adventures. At other times the narrator dreamed he was a sentinel whose boat would be rolling and pitching on the seas. As his boat smashed against frightening waves, the narrator came close to God and felt purified. The rocking and rhythmic sensations of the boat in general had not only a sexual significance for the narrator but closely resembled the motions of a baby being rocked and the feeling of comfort derived from rocking. In this instance, however, in the image of the heaving ship, he was confronted with brutal and uneven motions, feelings of distress, hatred, anxiety, and destruction. He was still identifying with the forces of the universe and still rebelling against them as a child who both loves and hates those upon whom he is dependent. "The sea howled. I was sure that nothing could happen since I was with these people who loved me. . . . Anger fills our sails" (*M,* 136).

The wind in the dream changed the sea's pace. It reflected the narrator's inner tempos: the sad sea, the placid sea, the smashing sea. It was personified: "Anger fills our sails. . . . The wind knocked against our sails. . . ." The wind represented the spirit of creation or the flow of the unconscious thrusting itself forward with all of its energy upon the conscious mind. The white sails stood for purity and for the spirit, which is frequently victimized by the power and the drive of the creative force. The wind on the ocean that was described forced the boat into storms or onto reefs. The wind blew with such force that the men fell onto the decks and then overboard. Suddenly, in the midst of this whirlwind tempo or burst of creative energy, the narrator had an extraordinary vision. A head appeared with curly hair, a sailor trembling in the wind and fog. And the boat moved ahead framed in haze. Strangely enough, the narrator's vision of the young boy with curly hair was an exact replica of the face Bulkaen had had tatooed on his left shoulder, unknown to the narrator at the time of the vision. A parallel can be drawn between the face the narrator saw in the haze of the foaming sea and Christ—as a hero and god-man.

The narrator's affinity with Christ, also a pariah who was punished for his audacity in that he broke with traditions, went still further in another dream. The narrator was aboard a galley on a warm, flat sea. In the nude, he was ascending a mast that looked like a cross, and the crew looked up at him, forming a circle below. The captain walked out on the deck but did not want to disturb the narrator's tormented ascension, and just as he was about to reach the top of the mast, he fell. The next morning, in the dream, he was awakened in the captain's arms.

The narrator wanted to climb the mast. Such an endeavor indicates an identification with Christ climbing the cross. This *imitatio Christi* was too much for a human being to bear. The fact that he almost reached the top of the mast or cross, that is, the central point of the circle in his dream, meant that he had almost fulfilled his spiritual aspirations. He fell because what he wanted to do, or the state he wanted to reach, was not psychologically possible or real. The fall also indicated a serious alienation between his conscious and unconscious attitudes—between spirituality and sexuality.

The narrator seemed to be torn between two opposites: the pure spirituality of the saint that would amount to a crucifixion and instinctuality. This pull of opposites, noted by Heraclitus and referred to as enantiodromia in psychological terminology, occurs when one side of a pair of opposites is overly activated in the personality. Enantiodromia is the sudden switch to the oppostie attitude, the swing of the pendulum from one extreme to the other. This polarity that the narrator experienced resulted in his fall from an overly spiritual attitude, as witnessed by the climbing of the mast, to the overly sexual attitude that resulted in his awakening in the arms of the captain. It is also demonstrated a need to be mothered, held, and embraced, which is part of the dynamism of the homosexual.

The heights the narrator reached in his dream by climbing the mast also represented his inability to face his own inner weaknesses. These he tried to bury within himself. As he wrote: "I had to at all costs dissimulate my profound weakness. . . ." He did not want to show the other convicts his overly sensitive or, as he put it, his weak side. He must appear "strong," "hard," and "brave"—the opposite of what he was. And so at night, in order to escape from the arduousness of maintaining a front, he would slip into his "dream-boat" and sail away on his "night sea journey"—the night light in the prison becoming the ship's lantern, the ground swell of the boat marked by the hall bell, the whispering of the convicts becoming the hushed admiration of the crew, and the storm at sea brought about by his unbridled feelings.

The narrator's inner world, as revealed in the previous dreams, indicated that he was still very much a part of the convict world, still faceless, a victim of his instincts and his unconscious. If his situation were not to change, he would be like the ship about which he dreamed and would be pushed here and there by the torrential sea. He might even sink beneath the sea, which would mean in psychological terms the engulfing of his conscious attitude by his unconscious, that is, he would become psychotic. And there he might lie forever, in oblivion. The fact that his ship (in image form) pushed forward, however, in its quest for freedom, implied by extension that growth had begun.

Since Genet's characters are, he tells us, extensions of himself, we can conclude that the author at this period was struggling for survival, that he was also laying the groundwork (unconsciously) for his future life as a writer. Only years later did Genet realize, he wrote, that both at Mettray and at Fontevrault, his life had been rooted in the dream: "And as at Mettray, I had the feeling that the dreams had not sprung from nothing—as dreams seem to do—I have just had the feeling that the entire part of my life had deep roots in this dream" (*M*, 308). It was through the dream, then, and the "miracle" (that will now be analyzed), that Genet became aware of the fact that the material from which his books would be made, would come from himself *alone.*

The Miracle

The miracle that Genet experienced at Fontrevault and as related by the narrator in the *Miracle of the Rose* can be interpreted in many ways. Jacques Derrida reacts to the dream sequence by observing that "the text itself obliges us to draw on this language: this dream is a dream within another dream, and within the dream of another. That, the miracle of the rose, which can take place only in a text, as text, implies a certain chaining of the critical body."[6] As an imagistic transposition of a new attitude, the dream is premonitory in nature: it reveals the various steps and stages involved in the birth of Genet, the artist.

The miracle revolved around a fellow inmate Harcamone, whom the narrator had known at Mettray.[7] When he saw him again at Fontevrault, he was struck by his hero's beauty and power. He felt that he was looking up at an "exceptional" being, a god, and was "dazzled" by his presence. He wanted to kneel before him and put his hands over his eyes to prevent their exposure to Harcamone's "fire," which might blind him. The narrator was unconsciously acting out the role of the passive penitent groveling before his active god.

Harcamone was awaiting execution at Fontevrault for two murders he had committed, the first when he was sixteen years old and the second, fifteen years later. The first murder was caused by Harcamone's "timidity," the narrator explained. He had tried to make love to a ten-year-old girl he had accompanied to a field and who had permitted him to stroke her long hair. When she suddenly fought him off, he strangled her. Harcamone's second murder consisted in killing a prison guard, the one who had been the nicest to him. Neither murder was premeditated.

The girl Harcamone had murdered is reminiscent of the ten-year-old girl whom Genet had loved and who had died and also of Solange, who had been sent away from Divine's home town in *Our Lady of the Flowers*. The age of ten, the time Genet first stole; the age of sixteen, when he was at Mettray; and the age of thirty-one, when Genet began to write, represent important stages in his life. During these three stages, Genet had either killed aspects of himself or they had seemingly disappeared from view: his feminine and tender self at ten symbolized by the girl Harcamone strangled; his inner child at sixteen; his adolescence at thirty-one.

Harcamone is a projection of the narrator: a compensatory image.[8] The narrator looked upon Harcamone's glory as inhuman: "crowning," "saintly," and "celestial." Harcamone had attained the stature of a divinity because he had overcome the fear of death and of the guillotine that awaited him. The narrator, his opposite, trembled at the thought of the guillotine, just as he shuddered at the thought of life—both fears being an expression of the same anxiety.

Harcamone, a god for the narrator, was a composite of opposites: the killer and the killed, the living and the dead, the good and the evil. Furthermore, Harcamone was completely free of guilt. He never once regretted the two murders. He had wanted to be a murderer, and this desire was so strong that he had sacrificed his life to attain his goal. The narrator, unlike Harcamone, was submerged in guilt feelings and was forever sacrificing and doing penance, thereby paying for the sin of being born.

The first miracle occurred when the narrator saw Harcamone, who was kept in solitary confinement except on special days, in the room reserved for shaving the inmates. Harcamone was weighed down with chains bound around his wrists and ankles. His curly hair had grown so long that it formed a halo around his head. The curls looked as though they twisted cruelly and resembled a crown of thorns. Suddenly, as the narrator was staring at this god, Harcamone was transformed. The chains that bound his wrists turned into garlands of white roses. The narrator felt illumined, like a religious fanatic who had kissed the coat, fingers, or relics of a saint or prelate. The narrator made his way toward his god, Harcamone. With a pair of scissors the narrator had been permitted to use to trim his nails, he cut off one of the most beautiful roses that had been attached to Harcamone's left wrist. The head of the rose fell on the narrator's naked foot and rolled on the floor. The narrator picked it up. He was both ecstatic and horrified; being suddenly aware of the omen—Harcamone's approaching death. When Harcamone saw the rose on the floor, he paled. Suddenly, the roses faded; Harcamone's smile returned; the chains reappeared; and the vision was over.

Genet's criminal or his "cult of the assassin"[9] must be looked upon in a broad and universal sense as a symbol of the transgressor who braves society's rigid laws. There is, then, an affinity in Genet's mind between this criminal and Christ, who also transgressed by upsetting the laws of the land when he promulgated his ideas. The narrator, and Genet by extension, therefore, sees in Harcamone (a projection of himself) a Christ figure. All three (Christ-Harcamone-Genet) were misunderstood by society, all three were pariahs. It is in the light of this analogy that the miracle will be interpreted.

The fact that Harcamone's curls turned into a crown of thorns is an indication of the world mocking him and trying to crush his kind. The chains transformed into white roses come to represent bondage, confinement, and society. They also indicate the narrator's limited and constricting conscious attitude, which seems to be overly earthbound at this point. These chains or earthly bonds that tie this godlike or transcendental spirit to the ground have been replaced by the "divine rose" or "heavenly rose," the feeling principle in man. Life, then, according to the image of the enchained Harcamone, can be experienced only in an imprisoning fashion because of the limitations imposed by the body. It is only in fighting against the bodily or the material aspects of life that such facets are experienced as imprisoning.

The foot upon which the rose has fallen, as that part of the body nearest the earth, has a generative significance. The rose then rolls to the ground. Such attention indicates a new inner development on the narrator's part. His spiritual self, which had been so alienated from reality that it could only live in a separate realm, in an imaginative world, will now, since it has fallen to the ground, derive greater strength from the earth or foot where it will henceforth find its nourishment. The narrator, as the vision indicates, is slowly becoming aware of his inner creativity, or his inner "wealth."

The second and more significant miracle occurred before Harcamone was to be guillotined. It must be recalled that in French prisons the condemned man never knows when he is to be executed. On the date set, the prison guards tiptoe into the victim's cell, grab him, shave his head, cut his collar, then walk him out at dawn to be guillotined in the presence of the chaplain and other prison officials. Since the doomed convict is not informed as to when his death will take place, his nerves are on edge. Whenever he hears footsteps in the prison corridors at night, he is seized with panic and wonders if it is his turn.

After Harcamone's trial, the guards took him to his cell. The narrator was haunted by Harcamone's presence. He had "visions" of this "Dalai-Lama," as he sometimes alluded to him. For forty days before Harcamone's death, the narrator seemed to have established some sort of occult rapport with him. Though they never saw each other during that period, the narrator could *see* into Harcamone's cell situated in some higher region in the prison. The narrator's emotional intensity had reached such a pitch that the last four nights before Harcamone was guillotined, by some inexplicable means, he was present in spirit in Harcamone's cell and *saw* everything that was going on:

> Harcamone was harrying me. . . . I haunted Harcamone more than he haunted me. I wanted to help him. He had to succeed. He had to keep his wits about him, to gather his power as one fathers a mob. He had to nourish himself so that his body would not be feeble. I watched over him, I tensed my mind. I stiffened it. I forgot whatever wasn't Harcamone and his flight from the physical world. . . . Finally on the fortieth night, I had a revelation; Harcamone's cell appeared within me. Wearing his shirt, he went to the window. It still seems to me that as he walked his whole being screamed. (*M*, 319)

On the fortieth night, as the narrator was lying on his bed, he felt a "clap of thunder" explode within him. All seemed to reel and become intoxicated about him; flowers, stars, seas, and mountains moved and burst into life. The narrator saw his god Harcamone and was with him. He watched him walk toward the window: "The moon was full. The window was open on a countryside livid with terror. I trembled lest he escape through the open wall, lest he call for held to his other in the stars and lest the sky crowd into the room and snatch him before my very eyes, to his other in the sea, and lest the sea come rushing in. From my cell I saw the helpless god's terrible and prodigious signal to the others of the night, to the doubles, to his lords, to himself away from here" (*M*, 319).

The narrator was suddenly panic-sticken because Harcamone was at the window ready to step into the night or to be called away by his family, the stars, and the heavens. Like Pascal, who trembled before the marvels of the world and its two "infinites," so the narrator was stirred with anguish. If Harcamone were to merge with everything around him, float here and there into the heavens, he would be doomed, symbolically speaking, to spiritual death.

The strange part of the narrator's vision was that he was both actor and spectator in his own drama. He was the narrator and also Harcamone. He saw Harcamone standing near the window, getting thinner and thinner, ready to slip through the bars, prepared to "aspire." Then, something snapped. Harcamone got down from the window ledge. He returned to the middle of his room. He would not seek to escape into the night. Such a turn of events implied that a change in direction was about to occur. The narrator (as projected onto Harcamone) would now seek an *inward* path and not an *outward* one in an endeavor to find his *way* in life.

The second and third nights the narrator spent with his "mystic fiancé" were even more disquieting. He saw Harcamone wait for the guard to fall asleep, then rise and walk toward the door. He had hardly gone three paces when the irons around his wrists and ankles opened and dropped noiselessly to the floor. Harcamone filled his lungs with air, pronounced an invocation and summoned all of his energy. The magical operation in which he was now indulging drained him of all his strength. But as a result of his ordeal, he succeeded in passing through his cell door. And as he crossed the door, his vestments were removed by some mysterious means, and Harcamone walked nude through the corridors.

The vision of Harcamone breaking through his cell door, which represented a penetration into a new dimension, and choosing to gain freedom through an inward thrust, that is, through the prison corridors rather than out of the window, implied that the narrator was now ready and willing to take this same step: to look within himself, to dredge up from the bottom of his being all those aspects of life that had tortured him, which he had formerly sought to escape through the adoption of either an overly spiritual or overly sexual attitude. The hero Harcamone would have to wander through the maze of corridors, just as any hero wanders through dangerous and confusing lands, until he found his hidden treasure, the self, and with this discovery, completeness. But wanderings and journeys if prolonged forever and without goals can also be dangerous and lead to eventual stagnation and disintegration.

The narrator's apocalyptic vision burst upon him like a visitor from another world. The fact that he could transport himself into Harcamone's cell, symbolizing a "containing" object, which is similar to a maternal vessel, implied that the narrator was going through a state of regression into the mother. Such a phase might be followed by rebirth and renewal. Harcamone's decision to go inward brings to mind the biblical story of Jonah, who was swallowed by the whale and who remained in the animal's belly for three days. A person who sinks into the fish's belly or into his childhood, his mother, his unconscious, or his cell, vanishes from the existing world. Yet in this deepest darkness he finds unexpected visions of world beyond and within himself. The narrator's unconscious depth had been reactivated by the thoughts surrounding Harcamone's execution, which he paralleled with his own psychological death. The narrator's fear of the guillotine has already been mentioned; it loomed large in the psychological picture. This fear of death is also a fear of life and of being cut off from life. The narrator seemed to have regressed within to his primal world. Here he would find the nourishment that would give him the strength, if not to overcome, at least to cope with his fear of death-life. In this state of regression, the narrator would either sink or swim. He would either remain in the whale's belly or be regurgitated by the animal. Since Harcamone was to die, those aspects the narrator projected onto him would be killed, and the rest of his personality would be released from the stranglehold his depths had upon him. But not yet, since Harcamone was still wandering about the prison corridors. He had passed through his cell door. Now he had to cross a second, more important door.

As the fatal night of the execution approached, the narrator felt Harcamone tensing up, struggling with himself. He had to find the secret of getting through the *second* door. What was behind the second door? Why was it so important? But Harcamone could not break through that all-important door.

The narrator experienced his greatest revelation when he saw the sleeping Harcamone awaken when four black-clad men (a lawyer, a judge, an executioner, and a chaplain)[10] entered his room. Harcamone decided, however, to return to his state of semislumber. He rose in this condition, and the narrator saw him suddenly adorned in laces, silks, brocades, leather boots, blue silk pants, a cream-colored shirt open at the collar, a chain with a medal bearing the order of the Golden Fleece hung about his neck.[11] Harcamone began growing larger and larger until he exceeded the size of the cell, and "he burst it, filled the Universe. . . ." By the same token, the four men grew smaller until they resembled bedbugs. They began climbing up his leg. The judge and the lawyer penetrated Harcamone's body through his ear; the chaplain and the executioner "dared to penetrate through his mouth." As they walked around in the various canals and orifices of Harcamone's body, they cried out: "The heart, have you found the heart?"

The fact that Harcamone had grown to such an extent and was wearing royal vestments and a medal representing the order of the Golden Fleece signified an inflation of Harcamone's spiritual and physical sides, which were at odds with each other. The four men represented the limited categories of the conscious mind. These four men understood little of the conflict the narrator and his kind suffered, for they always remained on the surface of things. Though devoid of sensitivity, imagination, and understanding, they dared to penetrate the convict's or the god's deepest realms. The judge and the lawyer penetrated through the winding canals of the ear, its labyrinthine and confusing aspects, implying a disturbance within the rational conscious orientation. The chaplain and the executioner were paired off and entered through the mouth. They represented the lower or sexual aspects of the quaternity. The chaplain symbolized man-made aspects of religion with their circumscribed rules. Such a superficial attitude toward the divine would mean death to the soul.

The four men inside the body exploring Harcamone's interior finally came to a door faced with a mirror upon which was incised, with a diamond, a heart crossed with an arrow. The door opened into a cold, white room, in the center of which stood a sixteen-year-old boy playing the drum. The four men were getting closer and closer to the heart. Eros-Cupid had been there, as indicated by the heart and the arrow.

The heart is to be found where the hurt is. The drummer boy referred to Harcamone, who at sixteen killed, for erotic reasons, the ten-year-old girl. It was from this point on that he, the drummer or the child within the man, was enclosed, misunderstood, and imprisoned by society and forced to dwell in a cold white room, his personality icing up and becoming sterile because of it. The drum stood for Harcamone's heart, which had not ceaased pounding since the murderous act had been committed.

Another mysterious door now opened, and the four men entered a second room. They found themselves facing a rose that was monstrous in size and beauty. The chaplain knew he was looking upon the "Mystic Rose." He and his companions were dazzled by its splendor. They spread the petals of the rose. They had reached the heart of the rose. They peered down its center, which looked like a black hole, and as they did so, they were seized with vertigo and "fell into this profound look." They fell into their own image or the image they saw.

The four men who symbolized the conscious mind's attitude were hypnotized by the wealth of images or the storehouse of treasures they had just perceived in the heart of the rose or the self. They had seen what no mortal should see, what only God should behold—the depths of man, a world of primordial images. The conscious or rational mind as represented by the four social functions (values in society) was so dazzled by the splendor of the red rose and the riches it revealed that it lost its balance. Such social functions or social values as represented by the four men could not possibly be accepted or related to Harcamone's unconscious attitude. They were lost in the process and because of that, values collapsed, notions died, and alienation ensued.

On the following night, the narrator again saw Harcamone in his vision. He was being led to the guillotine at dawn by the executioner, the lawyer, the judge, and the chaplain. Harcamone's agony, which made a magnificent story, wrote the narrator, was born from the most pitiable moments of his (the narrator's) life and reminded him of a man condemned to death nearly two thousand years ago.

The underlying image in this last phase of the miracle symbolizes the sacrificial death and resurrection of Christ, conceived as the self-sacrifice of Harcamone, who accepted the consequences of his first and second crimes, just as Christ, by continuing his preachings against established religions, invited his own crucifixion. The breaking or ending of life signified the sacrifice of power or the sacrifice of the conscious attitude toward life that had been oriented in a certain direction. It is the entry into death, that land beyond the conscious or rational, which the self-sacrificing hero aims for. In this way, he attains immortality through rebirth.

The vision of deeper things, of primordial images and primitive forces that underly all life and are the nourishing and creative elements living in the heart of the rose, were made visible to the narrator's conscious mind through the four men. If the narrator were to become a self-sufficient individual and independent of others, he would have to break with his previous attitude of permanent identification with all that was about him. If the narrator allowed his psychic energy to stagnate in his prison environment, in his dream fantasies, or unconscious world instead of living life out, his growth would be stunted. His unconscious would keep re-creating the same milieu, *ad infinitum,* through projection. The narrator would be caught up in a whirlpool—seeking his own self in the center but never able to grasp its amorphous contours. His destiny would not lie in his own hands but those of strangers.

Christ suggested, as had Abraham and Moses before him, that each man ruthlessly separate or break with his family and environment in order to permit growth of self and independence of spirit and soul. Genet, as revealed through the characters, the symbolism, and the imagery in the *Miracle of the Rose,* was trying to effect just such a break with his substitute family, that is, his physical prison and its inmates, and life as he was living it in reality.

As a youth, he had appealed to his imagination in order to make his life a little more bearable. These reveries and dream fantasies had grown out of proportion; had taken a stranglehold on him and caused him to clothe Mettray and Fontevrault with a fabulous fairy-tale atmosphere. The miracle had been the vehicle for his withdrawal from the real prison atmosphere and entry into his inner world.

Before the miracle had occurred he had not been able to probe his depths and dredge up from the bottom of himself, from that "Realm of Darkness," as he called it, all those tangled feelings and threads of emotions he had only sensed vaguely. The miracle had yielded him sight: this sight had given him a new orientation that he expressed symbolically throughout the narrative. Genet could consciously—and with the objectivity of the artist—now carve from himself the work of art.

Chapter Four
Funeral Rites

> It is hard to be a leper and to carry the infamous wound with one and to know that one will never be cured of it and that nothing can do any good.
> But that each day it increases and penetrates more deeply, and to be alone and to bear one's own poison. . . .
>
> —Paul Claudel, *The Announcement Made to Mary*

The miracle that had caused Genet's descent into self and that he described in the *Miracle of the Rose* resulted in the emergence of a new attitude toward life. His present way of looking at things helped him to grapple with some of his obsessions, namely, evil and death, not intellectually, but by sifting the depths of experiences. From his immersion in life he learned that absolutes, either good or evil, do not exist, and paradoxically, that death is not an end, but rather an initiation into another realm of being.

Reactions to *Pompes Funèbres* (*Funeral Rites*), written in 1947, were mixed. Some critics referred to it as a masterpiece, others, like Philip Thody, denigrated the novel for its lack of structural cohesion and for what he called its "self-indulgent rhetoric." He did concede, however, that it had appeal for those "who, like Cocteau, place the highest value on the surrealist and irrational aspects of his work."[1] Camille Naish considered *Funeral Rites* "a metaphor for sodomy, a slow penetration into blackness corresponding to the narrator's defloration of his friend."[2] Jacques Derrida's circuitous deconstructionist appraisal of *Funeral Rites* reads as follows:

> Like the downshifting multiplication into a crowd of Johns (the author, the narrator, the narratee, the dead), the play of bands envelops the Gospel in its *Funeral Rites* and mimes the resurrection. . . . he writes his *Funeral Rites* and the remain(s): with the assiduous gestures of a philologist, an archeologist, a mythologist bent on dispersing, destroying, crossing out whatever he finds or reconstitutes. The most critical operation. But his assiduousness is strange, as if distracted from itself. He always seems in fact to be assiduous about some-

thing else, detached from what he does. He tells you another (hi)story, you follow the narrative attentively; he shows you this or that with a finger, and yet (this hanging counterpart) fucks (*enculé*) you, his eyes elsewhere. He thus fully comes (*jouit*), as in his paradigm, and thinks there 'I recognize a recurrence of my childhood love (*goûts*) of tunnels. I bugger (*enculé*) the world.' "[3]

The Turning Point

In *Funeral Rites* Genet adapts a more cerebral approach to the technical aspects of his work. The fresh and exciting spontaneity of *Our Lady of the Flowers* and the *Miracle of the Rose* has been tempered. The measured hand of the artist at work becomes more and more visible. Genet now takes infinite pains to build up his novel into groups of dramatic fragments, each of which seems to shoot into view at repeated intervals. Such a technique leads to the creation of a series of violent surprises, which leaves the reader gasping for breath.

What is new and of extreme interest in *Funeral Rites* is Genet's treatment of political forces: nazism, fascism, communism. Each of these political points of view comes into focus at a given moment; is scrutinized and dramatized from all angles by both the characters and the author, after which it is reflected over and over again as a mirror image. The events that come into being as a result of these various images take on mythlike proportions outlined by Antonin Artaud in his theatrical scenario *The Conquest of Mexico.* Myths, universal forces, must mingle their enmities on stage, Artaud wrote, until each fighting entity shatters and wounds the other. In this way, man will have been shocked into a new state of awareness, and his former point of view will no longer be stubbornly maintained. In a similar manner, Genet endows both historical and fictional reality with cataclysmic force. The reader, then, is swept along in this energetic flow and, *en passant,* is shattered, thereby broadening the limited vision of his or her early views. With the violence of the Marquis de Sade or of Lautréamont and with the lyrical power and passion of Jean Racine or Paul Claudel, Genet invites us to penetrate new dimensions with him.

Language is one of Genet's most potent tools for arousing his readers. The richness of the dissonances and polyphonies embedded in his text, the correspondences, insights, and images to which they give rise, in addition to the sudden metalepses and associations, endow Genet's text with a unique power of its own. A case in point occurs in *Funeral Rites,* when a prison chaplain discussing the fate of some convicts with the army captain who heads the firing squad, suddenly screams out the word "Dieu." The shock and clang effect is not only traumatic, but ironic and ambiguous as well, serving to usher in a whole series of sensations for the protagonists involved and for the reader. Questions are posed without being answered, thereby injecting suspense into the atmosphere. Was the chaplain conveying a sense of despair, surprise, anger, or supplication in his pronouncement? In the same scene, after repeating the word "revelation," this morpheme reverberates so powerfully in the priest's head that he is deprived momentarily of his ability to think. The spiritual presences associated with the words "Dieu" and "revelation" and the dissociation between the signs and empirical meanings connected with them, not only weigh heavily upon the proceedings, but increase an already unsettling ambiguity.[4]

Genet forces his heroes to act and react not only upon each other but upon the spectator as well. The reader then is pulled here and there by the sheer dramatic power of the novel's mythlike characters and events. With increasing horror or rapture, the reader watches as Genet backs away at each character's outer coverings in his intense desire to reach truth—to penetrate man's solitude.

The world Genet resurrects in *Funeral Rites,* with its "fabulous" aspects of evil and death, had been lived in by him years and years back during his "pilgrimage." It was a hauntingly depressing past, a world so ugly and sordid it could "freeze a dead person. . . ."[5] Such is the realm, wrote Genet "I am slowly bringing forth from myself, with the idea of turning it into a poem. . . ." It is a world that "lived within me, in a sunless countryside, without sky, without stars . . ." (p. 107).

Genet's ability to face his past seemed to have released him from bondage. Like Rimbaud and Claudel, Genet burst forth at this point in his life with a newfound freedom. He wrote as if a tidal wave had arisen within him. He felt exhilarated by his catharsis, imbued with audacity, Gidean fervor, and violence. "I am drunk with life," he wrote, "violence and despair" (*p,* 108). These emotions flowed with extreme mobility from jubilation to despair, tenderness to cruelty, evil to good. Such dynamism, because of its very intensity, could not last any length of time, for, as Baudelaire had remarked years before, its fire would have consumed the individual. There are, then, parts of *Funeral Rites* that are less vital, even static, making the subsequent upsurge of emotions by contrast that much more drastic.

Genet now saw the world within the framework of the work of art.

Writing had become something "sacred" for him. It had taken on an aura and though it was fraught with agony—the agony every artist knows only too well—Genet pursued it almost compulsively. The creative act, he was now coming to realize, fulfilled both an emotional and aesthetic need for him. The latter gave him an urge to create something of beauty, the former, to seek a way of life.

Genet had reached a turning point. He now knew that if he continued his criminal career he would remain stunted and unfulfilled. A choice, he unconsciously realized, now had to be made. Should he continue his criminal activities? Should he pursue his literary life? When writing, he confessed, he experienced a kind of *grace,* a feeling of airiness and lightheartedness. As a criminal he would be impelled to face the reality of his acts, to proceed with positive, measured, sober, practical steps. He would fail in his trade if he succumbed to the same giddy emotions he experienced when writing. Were he to give up writing, he would also have to abandon the state of grace that he seemed to need so desperately at this time.

But there was yet another alternative. Could Genet combine writing and crime? Make writing an act of aggression? In *Funeral Rites,* he attempted just such an achievement. "I have pillaged, stolen, betrayed" (*P,* 100), Genet wrote as he began his campaign to fight the reader (society), to inflict pain, suffering, trembling, and anger upon him.

The desire to shock and wound his readers was not an unusual outcome of the emotional difficulties Genet was now suffering. His inner search, after the "miracle," was to some degree an unconscious attempt to bring order to his disparate identities. By bringing his conflicting identities to light and life, Genet hoped to rid himself of certain characteristics that he considered undesirable (weakness) and take on other qualities (strength) that he idealized. He wanted to be the image he had created for himself, paralleling in some respects society's (mother's) rejection of him. This double rejection put him in a highly vulnerable position. Unable to relate properly to any part of his many identities, he underwent severe inner conflicts, which led to an attitude of violence, external and internal, murder and suicide: "I willed myself to be a traitor, a thief, a plunderer, informer, hateful, destroyer, disdaining, cowardly. By dint of hatchet strokes and screams, I cut the cords which bound me to the world of habitual morality, sometimes, I methodically undid the knots. Monstrously, I withdrew from you, from your world, from your cities, from your institutions" (*P,* 109).

Genet attempts to drag the reader down into the morasses of depravity, wounding him all the while, and from there to make him view the world—the traitors, the criminals, the poisoners, the torturers: Hitler, who mesmerized a whole nation into following him in his sordid ways, Catherine de Medici who, on Saint Bartholomew's Eve, feasted on Protestant blood and flesh. Genet not only inflicts his hatchet blows on his readers but provokes them to retaliate. He builds their hatreds and violence up to a peak while constructing his own at the same time.

The Narrative

Funeral Rites has a relatively uncomplicated plot. The author leaves the prison environment and introduces his readers to a Paris during the Liberation, to Hitler's Germany, to traitors, to patriots—and always to the homosexual. His heroes, though probably based on actual people, are fictionalized for the purpose of the novel. The narrative takes place in the two days after the fictional Jean Genet (who is the narrator of the story) saw his lover's body (Jean Decarnin, whom he had betrayed) lying in the coffin in the morgue from four in the afternoon until midnight the following day.

The character Jean Decarnin is a Communist member of the French Maquis,[6] who had been killed on a barricade by a member of the French Milice[7] during the Liberation of Paris on 19 August 1944. As the book opens, the fictional Genet (the narrator) is returning from the morgue where he had been taken by the maid Juliette, Decarnin's eighteen-year-old fiancée. Juliette is not only mourning her lover's death, but also that of the fifteen-day-old daughter she had supposedly had by Decarnin, but in reality by a captain of the French Milice. As the narrator makes his way back from the morgue, he is transfixed by the sight of an immense dark stone angel that seems to be rising up before him. He feels both attracted and repelled by it—horrified and in awe of what seems to be the "angel of death." Upon closer inspection, this apparition or premonition turns out to be the Trinity Church, and on its facade he discerns an eagle, that of the Reich, the force of evil stamped on a human institution—the Church.

The narrator's story involves characters other than Decarnin, whose heroic death is glorified in *Funeral Rites*. Erik Seiler (an anagram of Reich), the handsome German tanker who turns out to be the lover of Decarnin's mother and with whom the narrator falls in love; Paulo, a member of the French Milice and Decarnin's half-brother; Riton, also a member of the French Milice, who becomes Erik's lover; and the Berlin Executioner, Erik's lover.

Genet emerges as a conscious artist in *Funeral Rites*. A cleverness, perhaps a certain amount of insincerity now seems to have brushed away the naive candor of his first works. He appears to want to remain aloof, to trick and mock his readers into following him into his magic world of spiritual and sexual intoxication. Influenced by Proust, Joyce, and Kafka, Genet proceeds by flashback, fadeout, stream of consciousness, association, analogy, suggestion, the déjà vu, and a heavy impressionism. His images blend or fade into one another, merge, bring forth strange associations and sensations. Each picture billows forth and fades into the atmosphere like smoke. For example, Genet writes of a matchbox that he touched for the sensation it created within him. The sensation evoked an image that, by analogy, brought forth another. A certain character bumps his foot against a curb and is transformed into a young Nazi. The past, thereby, is recaptured just as Proust succeeded in resurrecting it with his "madeleine." Genet also has recourse to nature descriptions, introducing a thematic change. "The moon was veiled," he wrote, creating a feeling of mystery that is interrupted seconds later by the brutal eruption of reality.

As a writer, Genet began distinguishing between the novelist who can treat divers themes while developing with precision different character types, and the poet, whose art is more limited. Genet considered himself to be a poet and not a novelist. As a poet, he would have to follow the dictates of his heart and attract to himself all those beings marked with evil and misfortune. For this reason, he stated, all of his characters resembled each other, and the poems or songs they provoked emanated from the same source—his guts.

Evil versus Good

Funeral Rites is like a giant, heaving symphony in which evil and death, the two themes that haunt Genet, weave in and out. The question of good and evil obsessed Genet. Good and evil are opposite poles of a moral judgment that originates in man. Life, which is an "energetic process," needs these opposites because without conflict there can be no energy, no dynamism—hence, no life (*P,* 144). The fact that Genet felt this polarity between good and evil in such an excruciating manner made his existence all the more potent, his suffering all the more keen and inescapable. Genet would use this anguish to make his life more meaningful and to create his poem.

Genet sought to reach the forces which he called, in turn, good, God, self, mystic rose, inner deity—all of which come to signify wholeness or identity. If his goal could not be reached through the path we call "good," then he would pursue his course through the opposite, "evil." He hoped, unconsciously, by this means to unite opposites within himself and to create inner harmony.

Genet's odyssey as related in *Funeral Rites* would be dangerous. As the narrator, he would strain for the depths of degradation in order to attain its other side, that is, to experience God's grace. To put it in different terms, achieving the experience of the positive and fruitful forces of life would require merging with evil. The narrator would have to submit to and seek out all the ignominies known to man—his own version of Job's saga. Like the narrator, to a certain extent, Job's suffering was an initiation into a new world because the punishment God inflicted upon Job (the narrator upon himself) made him conscious of its opposite. He had to know Satan to know God. Dimitri in Dostoevski's *The Brothers Karamazov* also knew anguish. Father Zossima was aware of the heavy burden of pain Dimitri was to suffer, and when "he moved toward Dimitri . . . he sank on his knees before him . . . distinctly and deliberately bowed down at Dimitri's feet till his forehead touched the floor."[8] As a result of Dimitri's anguish new values emerged, mainly the lucid realization of his former acts, the acceptance of his personality as it was, including the bestial acts of which he was capable.

The narrator in *Funeral Rites* had mapped out a course as rigorous for himself as was Dimitri's or Job's. To endure self-imposed martyrdom required supreme heroism. To follow a path of evil, declared the narrator, would lead to solitude, to the solitaire, the diamondlike existence that is hard and sterile. To earn his solitude meant not only accepting the hatred and rejection of all humanity, but provoking it. The narrator's descent or ascent into evil would burn and scorch him with shame. When enduring it, he felt as though he were on fire, at once standing and lying on hot coals. In the depths of his being, however, after the outer core had gone up in smoke, his inner self remained unbruised, shining in its purity and beauty.

To what lengths would the narrator go in degrading himself? How deeply could he come to know evil? Betrayal, he wrote, had been the most difficult of all goals to attain and cost him the greatest efforts. He succeeded in becoming a traitor in *Funeral Rites,* he wrote, the day he had the courage to deliver over the friend he loved to the police. As a result of the suffering that followed this act, he learned the depths of his love for his friend: "Like good, evil is earned, little by little by a clever discovery which makes you slide vertically far from men, but most frequently by minute, daily, slow, deceiving work" (*P,* 52).

Evil in all forms and shapes graces *Funeral Rites.* As the character Hitler, created in *Funeral Rites,* evil stands out "resplendent." Hitler, "that fabulous emblem of a people delegated by Satan," sparkled like a diamond in his "glacial and solitary solitude," wrote the narrator. Hitler had transformed an entire nation. He had made evil triumph.

The narrator, living in Nazi Germany under the Hitler regime, did not stand apart. He was, in other words, not one evil being in a country of good people, but one evil being in a country of evil people and as such was accepted. He was, therefore, not a pariah and could not consider such an attitude of acceptance part of his trial. Since evil was relative and the Germans considered evil good, the narrator would then be considered good. He was not the butt of hatred. He could not win infamy in Germany since the Germans bathed in it like "fish in water. . . ." The narrator, therefore, returned to France where he would be considered evil. His initiation into evil required that he be hated by his own people, betray his own country, family, friends—sever all human bonds, become the object of disgust—even to the reader.

Decarnin, the central character in *Funeral Rites,* represents the forces of good. He is a courageous patriot. He hates the Germans, and his attitude toward them is unbending. He feels that the "least kindness toward them, the least nice word" might lead the enemy to believe that he is weak. Decarnin, in some respects, is Genet as an adolescent. Both Decarnin and Genet present a bold front to the outside world. This rigidity of attitude is characteristic of many of Genet's heroes: Harcamone, Bulkaen, Decarnin, for example, who fears (as Genet feared) that understanding and kindness—humanity, in short—implies weakness. A mask, then, is always worn by Genet's characters. Intrusion by the outside world into their private domain was strictly forbidden.

Decarnin, the symbol of good, is killed in *Funeral Rites.* Such an act indicates the temporary end of good in the world. Consequently, the invasion of evil in various incarnations stalks the pages of the book: Decarnin's Mother, Erik, the Executioner, Paulo, Riton. These phantoms emanating from Genet's unconscious are to be objects of beauty and admiration as well as of scorn and horror.

Decarnin's Mother is an example of the archetypal[9] son killer. She is like Ernestine in *Our Lady of the Flowers.* In *Funeral Rites,* the Mother takes her son's enemy, Erik, as her lover. She was never considered by Decarnin as a real mother. She even denied her relationship with her offspring when she said: "Me, I am Madame." She is drawn in vague strokes and never becomes a clear being. She remains an impersonal function, a symbol of the vengeful mother archetype.

Juliette, Decarnin's fiancée, is in some respects the image of the good woman who suffers because of life's misfortunes. She is reminiscent of Solange in *Our Lady of the Flowers.* But Juliette was not completely good, first, because she had led Decarnin to believe that he was the father of her child when he was not. Second, Juliette gave birth, and this act in itself was, according to the narrator, ugly and evil. A mother giving birth to a child was merely getting rid of a monstrous growth of flesh, a type of "unclean and reddish excrescence."

Erik is portrayed with greater clarity than either of the two women. In the novel, the narrator meets Erik Seiler, the handsome Nazi tanker, at Decarnin's mother's apartment. Upon his fourth visit, the narrator is so mesmerized by Erik that he divests himself of his own personality and dons Erik's, "I sunk into his past" (*P,* 24).

There is a flashback at this point to Erik's youth in Germany. The reader sees Erik (or is it the narrator projecting himself into Erik) sitting under a tree. He is naive. The Berlin Executioner comes up to him. The Berlin Executioner possesses the young boy. After a two-year relationship, Erik begins to take on the hard and brutal personality of his lover, while the Executioner becomes a softer human being. Erik no longer feels any link with humanity. In a supreme show of daring and power, he murders a fifteen-year-old boy who was playing with his dog in a field. Murder, wrote the narrator, is the symbolic act of evil and renders all other acts futile by comparison.

Since Erik was evil, the narrator wondered how he could have loved this man who was Decarnin's enemy: "Was it possible for me to accept without being torn asunder, into my intimate life one of those against whom Decarnin had fought until death?," asked the narrator (*P,* 12). Yes, it was possible. The narrator was continuing along the path he had mapped out for himself. But, had the narrator reached his goal of immersion into absolute evil, then his question would have been useless. He still had a long way to go.

Both Erik and the Executioner are projections of the narrator. The narrator is the adolescent Erik sitting under a tree, which, symbolically, shields and protects him from the sources of life. He is also the Executioner, who is double—brutish, on the outside, weepy (he is compared to a weeping willow tree), on the inside. The more the Executioner gets to know Erik, the more he divests himself of his mask; the more sensitive he reveals himself to be, the greater is his sadness. After Erik has met with the hard shell of life as symbolized by the Executioner's role in society, he loses his adolescent vulnerability. When Erik kills the fifteen-year-old boy, he almost fulfills the narrator's conceptions of ideal evil. But he falls short of his goal since he cannot accept the full impact of his act. He suddenly becomes aware of the fact that his "return to earth would be terrible" (*P,* 70).

Paulo, Decarnin's half-brother and a member of the French Milice, is another evil emanation. Paulo is what the narrator would have liked to have been: ruthless, cruel, impervious to hurt—a murderer. As a Milicien and so a traitor, he is even more vicious. He is an "instrument of torture," the narrator wrote, the most monstrous of nightmares. When Paulo passes by his brother's coffin, he is devoid of feelings. His complexion takes "on the color of a dangerous liquid" (*P,* 35). Paulo is a witches brew, a frightening mixture of evil-smelling chemicals and poisons infiltrating easily and painlessly into both animate and inanimate objects. Paulo is not going to die. He is made of matter—of "crystals"—and is *pure* evil.

Riton, another member of the French Milice, is also evil. One day, when the narrator drops into a movie he sees on the screen a sixteen- (or seventeen-) year-old lad, a Milicien, shooting a French Maquisard on the barricades. The audience in the theater screams with anger, whistles, and boos whenever the Milicien appears on the screen. As for the narrator, "his hatred for the Milicien was so strong, so beautiful that it was equivalent to the most solid love." And so, paradoxically enough, he hoped that it had been the Milicien who had killed Decarnin (*P,* 37). To love what everyone hates is part of the narrator's credo. The conflict of opposites, love-hate, makes the narrator's excitement still more acute, his fire still more scalding.

The narrator closes his eyes in the theater. He visualizes another scene, Decarnin being shot by Riton. He is bewitched by Riton's beauty, different from Decarnin's, and is "illuminated by an inner light," a strange sensation. He realizes that "A little love had passed on to Riton. I really had the impression that his love flowed from me, going from my veins, to his" (*P,* 108). The narrator reaches a state of ecstasy. "Riton, Riton," he says to himself, "but you can kill him, my boy! My darling! Kill him!" The narrator, his eyes still shut, watches the blood lust grow. The chase is on, Riton running along the rooftops in search of Decarnin in order to kill him. At this instant, the narrator realizes he loves both Riton and Decarnin and that an inner wedding ceremony is taking place between two facets of his own personality. When Riton finally kills Decarnin, the narrator is elated over the violence of the scene. His love for Decarnin's heroism in facing death is all the more profound.

The adventure the narrator had tried to live, that of being hated and hating, had been an arduous one requiring daring and strength. In the Miliciens, Erik and Paulo, he seemed to have found his ideal. They possessed the most vicious traits of any of the beings he had known, and for this reason he loved them. The Miliciens had cut all ties. "They were not only hated, but vomited up. I love them." No friendships were possible among the members of the Milice since they would betray anyone and everyone. They were "cursed like reptiles, they had taken on the mores of reptiles." They had dared "brave the disdain of public opinion" and so bathed in a "halo of shame." They had severed relations with family, friends, country—and disdained death (*P*, 51). The narrator, as projected into the Miliciens, had earned his solitude and his heroism. He had merged, as much as it was humanly possible, with evil.

Death

The second most important theme in *Funeral Rites* is that of death. Indeed, this work, wrote the narrator, is devoted "to the cult of a dead man." Genet's fear of death was so obsessive, as had been his fear of evil before he had immersed himself into it, that he felt impelled to devote an entire book to it.

In psychological terms, a fear of death indicates a fear of the decay or dissolution of one's personality. Genet's obsessive fear indicated, to a certain degree, his inability to discover his own "river bed." Until now he had been living only a provisional life in which his potential was not being fulfilled. His extreme pessimism points in part to this attitude when he writes: "Since my life has no meaning and a gesture signifies nothing, I want to stop living." Genet vacillated, as had Faust, from one pole to the other, from the heights of jubilation to the depths of despair. In such states of depression, Genet's gestures became empty, automatic, devoid of meaning.

In *Funeral Rites* Genet tries to face death, to understand it and accept it. He projects himself into the character of the narrator with this in mind. At Decarnin's funeral services, for example, he peers into his friend's coffin and feels as though he were looking directly at himself at that age, and his pain doubles. He describes his turmoil. He realizes that to dwell and mourn a dead friend (one's dead past), as he was now doing, makes him nostalgic and intensifies his anguish. The narrator tells of his pain in terms of a burning image: he feels as though the outer rim of his eyelids are on fire. This image indicates that all vision, both outer and inner, is going to be cut off if his attitude toward himself and life is not altered. Pain and confusion blur the differences he now establishes between the dead Decarnin (the boy the narrator used to be) and the mature narrator (writing the book) weeping over his own boyhood. If the narrator continues to smoulder in this state of ambivalence, that is, wishing to wipe out his adolescence while at the same time narcissistically conjuring it up, such fruitless activity would lead to the dissolution of his personality or the death of that personality. The symbol of death as revealed in *Funeral Rites* indicates the narrator's extreme fear of the decay of his being.

The narrator's fear of death progresses in intensity as the novel sweeps along. He sees death all about him: in trees, in a mutilated body, in church services, in rituals, in the mourning of Christ, in sacred objects. Indeed, he describes the unexpected feelings that overwhelm him as he kneels to pray during Decarnin's funeral. A cloud suddenly passes over the entire church, clothing it in darkness. At this instant, the narrator feels himself to be in direct rapport with God, to melt under his gaze. Suddenly he is transformed into a child who is praying fervently: "I am a poor child. Keep me from the Devil and from God. Let me sleep in the shade of your trees, of your convents, of your gardens, behind your walls. My God, I have pain" (*P*, 21). He asks for God's comfort. Because of his empathy, he feels two beings palpitate and burst with life within him—the adolescent and the elder. He calls these two beings, plus the presence of deity within him, a "pregnancy." Decarnin (the narrator as the adolescent) is one parent; the narrator (the elder) is another; and the third force is the transpersonal deity (which passes at this moment from the outer to the inner being of man). These three forces gave birth, symbolically speaking, to the *book*. The book then had traversed the path from death to life. The book is the offspring, the result of the inner activity of the three forces.

The narrator, then, has discovered how to transmute dead matter into living matter. Such an ability made him God, the creator, and man, the procreator. "I was certain of being God," he wrote, "I was God." To make certain he manipulated the destinies of his creations with dexterity he felt he would have to assimilate, to contain within himself, all of these beings. He could absorb their spirit and power sexually by making love to his creations as he had with Decarnin before his death or, through communion, by eating them, either actually as Riton had eaten the cat and as is done in primitive tribes, or symbolically, through communion.

As the narrator takes communion in church, he symbolically devours Decarnin's flesh and blood, thereby incorporating into himself "the only lover who had really loved me." It is a painful task, he writes. "To eat an adolescent killed on the barricades, to devour a young hero is not an easy thing. We all love the sun. My mouth is a mass of blood, and my fingers. I slashed the flesh with my teeth. Usually corpses do not bleed, yours did" (*P,* 13). The narrator is now like the cannibal eating his victim, dancing about the fire in the dark, experiencing an orgy of incantation.

After the ordeal of assimilation another awaits him: resurrection and incarnation. The belief of raising the dead goes back to antiquity. Coronation ceremonies, initiation rites, totemism, the enthronement and rulership of the sun (Osiris) and the Christian Incarnation are examples of this concept. These ritualistic ceremonies have a common denominator between them: the god is reincarnated into the initiate or the risen one and finds in him his new home.[10]

Genet had discovered his own past as had Baudelaire before him. It contained his "inner cemetery," his realm of the dead which he resurrected. It was in this deepest part of himself that his fantasies burgeoned and bits of his being visited and haunted him. In these depths, he wrote, "these years have deposited a mud in which bubbles appear. In each bubble lives a single *will to be,* which develops, becomes deformed, transformed, alone and according to the other bubbles, and forms an irridescent, violent ensemble, manifesting a will which has emerged from this mud" (*P,* 144).

Phantoms, then, in the form of mud bubbles emerged from what Genet termed "limbo," a region of imperfect and badly formed but malleable bodies that felt like the little clay figures children mold. When their time is up, these eerie half-beings—vampires in a certain sense—make their way back into the mud caskets from whence they came and there lie dormant until they are called upon to rise once again and dwell in the land of the living.

Genet dissected the feelings of these half-beings engendered within him with almost medical precision. He, the creator now, was also the objective analyst splitting down, slicing up a human personality in an endeavor to examine that being from all angles, ruthlessly and tenderly. Then, as though he had understood what was to be, by using some magic gesture, his personalities were put together again in a different and more comprehensive way, one more satisfying to their author.

To sweep into the realm of the "inner cemetery," to drench oneself in it, permitted Genet to establish a rapport with it. "Jean [Decarnin] will live through me," the narrator wrote. "I shall lend him my body. Through me he will act, think. Through my eyes he will see the stars. . . . I am assuming a very serious role" (*P*, 49). Genet's understanding of evil (and its opposite, good) and of death (as an initiation from one phase of existence to another), permitted him to gain the proper perspective and objectivity over his own being, so that he could play the role of creator and actor in the inner dialogue which is *Funeral Rites*.

Chapter Five
Quarrel of Brest

And, Sir, a novel is a mirror carried along a high road. At one moment it reflects to your vision the azure skies, at another the mire of the puddles at your feet. And the man who carries this mirror in his pack will be accused by you of being immoral! His mirror shows the mire, and you blame the mirror! Rather blame that high road upon which the puddle lies, still more the inspector of the roads who allows the water to gather and the puddle to form.

—Stendhal, *The Red and the Black*

Querelle de Brest (Quarrel of Brest), written in 1947, focuses on the sea, sailors, and murder. It takes the reader out of the prison atmosphere, out of the realm of the dead, and thrusts him into a seaman's world. That Genet should concentrate on the sea is not surprising in view of the fact that so much of his imagery in the *Miracle of the Rose* revolved around it.

Unlike Victor Hugo's or Pierre Loti's humanitarian and exotic treatment of sailors and the sea, Genet introduces his reader to a realistic group of rough and sordid seamen and their entourage. The prostitutes, murderers, and thieves who roam through his work are also poles apart from the underworld of, for example, the nineteenth-century Eugène Sue or the twentieth-century Francis Carco or Pierre Mac Orlan. The latter writers make the vice-ridden side of life so attractive to the reader that he feels empathy and pangs of nostalgia for the protagonists. Not so for Genet's characters, who are brutal, tortured, sadistic, divided human beings, forever vomiting out their wrath, their hatreds, their bitterness in scatological, pornographic, and bruising tirades. These beings repel, yet in some strange and haunting manner, they fascinate, appealing to some "unknown" element within man.

Genet uses Flaubert-like accuracy to describe his beings both inwardly and outwardly. In this way, he maintains the force and intrinsic power of each word, never overemphasizing by false and artificial brutality or cruelty any part of his narrative. Words are also used by Genet to create ample and varied rhythmic effects, thereby increasing the visceral attachment between the reader and the characters depicted.

The Narrative

Quarrel of Brest is the most complicated of Genet's narratives. He continually breaks up consecutive action and abolishes time and space by interrupting and paralleling sequences of events. Such rhythmic and spatial changes as he brings about create extreme multiplicity and fragmentation, a literary device by which the chaotic nature of his own emotions becomes manifest.

The novel concentrates on homosexuality, "love against nature."[1] Genet writes on the very first page of his narrative that he is addressing the homosexual. Indeed, this book delves more deeply into the subject of perversion than any of his previous works.

Quarrel of Brest takes place in Brest, an important military and commercial port in northwest France, situated on the left bank of the river Penfeld. Brest is a city of "fog and granite." The almost constant drizzle paints the scenery in gray, black, and white tones. The atmosphere is thickly depressing. Through this natural veil, which lends mystery to the city, the visitor can make out Roman vestiges and feudal fortresses.

The hero is George Quarrel, a sailor, murderer, thief, and opium smuggler who has arrived in Brest on the ship *Avenger*. Tobert, his brother, whose resemblance is so striking that they can hardly be distinguished form each other, is Mme Lysiane's lover. Mme Lysiane is the owner of "La Féria," the city's solemn and regal bordello.

Quarrel comes ashore to Brest. He has arranged that a sailor friend, Vic, will smuggle a package of opium into town for him. After Vic has completed his mission, Quarrel murders him. Quarrel sells the opium to Nono (Norbert), Mme Lysiane's husband. He then gives himself sexually to his "executioner," Nono, in order to expiate his crime.

Later, Quarrel has homosexual relations with Mario, the police chief, a frequent visitor at the bordello. Mario has a double, Marcellin, who is like an "excrescence." Mario, however, loves the sixteen-year-old Dédé. Dédé is also double. He robs with the thieves and then he denounces them, informing Mario of their crime.

Gil, an eighteen-year-old Pole, works in the dockyards. He loves and is loved by the fifteen-year-old Roger. The forty-five-year-old Théo also works there and is infatuated with Gil, whom he tries to dominate. Gil resents Théo's attitude because it prevents him from loving Roger completely. To right a wrong situation, Gil murders Théo. He hides out in an abandoned prison.

The police accuse Gil of having murdered both Vic and Théo. Quarrel is fascinated by the fact that Gil, like himself, has murdered. He feels a mystical bond between himself and Gil. In order to sanctify his thefts and murders (Quarrel has committed more than one murder before the story opens), Gil must be sacrificed. Quarrel convinces Gil to leave his hideout. He buys him a ticket for Bordeaux, betrays his activities to the informer Dédé, who calls the police. Gil is arrested as he is about to step onto the train for Bordeaux.

Lieutenant Seblon, who keeps a diary that is quoted occasionally, loves Quarrel. His love, however, is never realized, since he feels he must maintain face in a world that frowns on homosexuality. Lieutenant Seblon is never himself. On the outside he is respectable; on the inside he is a pervert, and thus he is unworthy of the society with which he wants to merge. His agony will be the most profound. Gil will be crucified physically; the Lieutenant, emotionally.

Multiplicity and Unity

The problem of multiplicity is treated in great detail in *Quarrel of Brest* because the homosexual, the main subject of the narrative, never really knows who he is. He is faceless. What the world sees is his mask, a male body that clothes a female inner being. This dualism, manifesting man's opposition within himself, becomes acute in *Quarrel of Brest*. It reaches the point, in fact, where it is expressed by building up a series of doubles: in historical and architectural descriptions, in events (two murders, two mystical experiences), in characters (two brothers, two policemen), contrasts between sea and land, freedom and captivity, and so forth.

There is a double pediment and double coat-of-arms, for example, on what used to be a prison located right outside of Brest. It is in this abandoned prison that Gil hides before Quarrel betrays him. Thereafter, the double coat-of-arms and double pediment is woven into the story and symbolizes the conflict with Gil. It also serves to point up the duality in other characters who come near its sturdy walls.

This double coat-of-arms, made up of the fleur-de-lys, a symbol of France, and the Ermine, that of Brittany, was created when Anne of

Britanny[2] married Charles VIII of France and later Louis XII, also king of France. These weddings brought about a political union between the kingdom of France and the duchy of Brittany. Genet wove some of this history into his narrative and thereby established a link with his country's past, and so with his own.

Genet compares the double coat of arms on the pediment to two halves of the fabulous egg laid by Leda after she had known Jupiter disguised as a swan. Both halves of this egg contained the seeds of supernatural strength and richness. From these eggs were born Castor and Pollux, the temporal and nontemporal aspects of the psyche. Such power as was vested in these eggs was also intrinsic to the prisoners who once inhabited this prison. Though they were enchained and considered dead to society, they still possessed the "germ," that inner fire that is the source of strength, creativity, and a life lived intensely.

Each character in *Quarrel of Brest* is double. Quarrel and Robert, his brother whom he resembles, had been one at birth, but split at the age of fifteen when Quarrel decided to become a thief. Quarrel represents the man of action, the criminal, the active homosexual. Robert symbolizes the inactive partner who accepts society but is detached from it. His passivity is such that he never really emerges as a character in the book. As for Quarrel, even his name implies dissension.

Mario, the chief of police, like all chiefs of police according to Genet, is both passive and active, depending upon the company he keeps. Once, when Mario is with Quarrel, for example, he entices him to describe his sexual relations with Nono. Mario's excitement grows to such a pitch that he feels the courage to provoke Quarrel to a fight.

Mario works in cahoots with the sixteen-year-old Dédé, who loves him and admires him for his strength. Dédé has given up his personality to serve Mario. When Dédé kneels down before his hero and kisses him, he looks, Genet writes, like a young female saint full of grace.[3] At these moments, the chief of police feels as though he is being burned by bits of fire, stabbed by flames. As Mario experiences the stigmata brought forth by Saint Dédé, his countenance alters. He becomes immovable as a rock. He reigns supreme.

But there are other moments, when Mario needs the accouterments of his profession or institution to hide behind for protection—the sun, the knife. Mario has, in fact, a host of weaknesses. Such characteristics are revealed at one point when he fears reprisals from a recently released dock worker. The anguish Mario experiences makes him aware of the façade behind which he seeks protection, the institution of the police.

What is this institution? Is it any more solid than the Navy? the Church? the Law? What Mario runs to for protection is a collective image, an institution which is in reality made up of a group of "human weaknesses" (*Q*, 206).

Nono is double. He is Mme Lysiane's cuckolded and passive husband. He is also the active opium smuggler and the active male homosexual who possesses Quarrel. He is no more able to face himself than are Quarrel or Mario. Nono's positive activity results from a feelng of anger and a desire for revenge. He wants to have sexual relations with his wife's future lovers before they cuckold him. In this way, he thinks, he will rid himself of his feeling of uselessness and shame.

Gil is another multiple personality. He walks through the narrative "in a universe where forms are still in a larval-like state" (*Q*, 239). Gil loves the fifteen-year-old Roger, but is dominated by Théo, a forty-five-year-old mason. Gil has to act, otherwise Théo will stifle him. His excuse for killing is that he cannot love the fifteen-year-old Roger as he wants to unless he is free from Théo's domination. Actually, he fears his own weakness and impotence. One evening, accompanied by Roger, he finds Théo at a table in a bar. He goes up to him, speaks a few words, breaks a bottle standing on the table, and with a piece of glass from it, cuts Théo's carotid. Those present are so stunned that they do not react, and Gil escapes into the night. Gil has asserted himself. His act, based on anger at his own impotence, has made of him an active individual. After the murder, however, he returns to his former state of passivity. He flees into the forest and is unwilling to bear the penalty of his act.

Lieutenant Seblon is, in many ways, the most pathetic and solitary character in the book. He is always masked, never himself. Outwardly, he is a manly type—handsome, blond, muscular. Inwardly, he is a homosexual in love with Quarrel. He does not live out his desires in actuality but rather records them in his diary, which is quoted now and then throughout the narrative. He always tries to hide his femininity behind a facade of harshness. He is puritanical with his crew. He never smiles. Secretly he wants to possess all his sailors, and Quarrel, in particular. Each sailor is a fragment of the perfect sailor, Quarrel, who incarnates the entire navy.

Lieutenant Seblon has to pay for his deceit at the end. Shame will be his means of earning forgiveness. Like Sainte Marie Alacoque or Saint Benoît-Joseph Labre,[4] Seblon practices humility and detachment to the point of refusing to give his body the most basic care. In the same spirit he choses a form of sacrifice. He walks alone along a road, opens his shirt, and lies down and rests his naked belly on excrement. He rises and continues his walk—like a leper. When humiliation has reached its keenest point, he realizes that "every birth in a stable is a grandiose sign . . ." (*Q*, 344). "It is thanks to Jesus that we can magnify humility since he made of it the sign of divinity. . . . And humility can be born only from humiliation. If not it is false vanity" (*Q*, 343). Lieutenant Seblon has reached the saint's state. He continues his walk and murmurs: "I infect! I infect the world" (*Q*, 344). Suffering and shame have been his. He has hung on the cross of life and has agonized, and because of this has been redeemed.

Quarrel of Brest is the story of man divided, of man against himself. As such the number "2" figures throughout the work in one way or another. Dualism or the number "2," according to medieval natural philosophers, indicated the presence of the Devil, who was emancipated on the second day of creation. On that day God separated the upper and the lower waters and for the first and last time, omitted after his work had been done, that "it was good." Multiplicity, separation, and opposition—all associated with the Devil—resulted from God's omission.

Quarrel, suffering from his dualism or multiplicity within his character, longs to be whole, to do as all the other characters in *Quarrel of Brest,* who are in actuality splintered facets of the hero's personality. Quarrel seeks, therefore, by means of a superhuman act or mystical experience to overcome all opposing forces within himself and recapture his original unity and well-being. Such an endeavor really belongs to the realm of the mystic who seeks to "empty himself," according to Mahayana Buddhism, of all mental contents and create a "void" within. According to Hebrew and Christian mystics, what is left within is called God. The melting away of one's own personality, in an attempt to experience the infinite, means unlimited perception and an actual disappearance of one's own personality. Genet's hero, Quarrel, experiences this feeling on two occasions. Such disappearance of individuality, or the achievement of complete detachment, means an obliteration of multiplicity and the discovery of "self" or "undifferentiated unity."[5] In the *Miracle of the Rose,* the narrator had almost described such a mystical experience when he found he was able to see into Harcamone's cell. In *Quarrel of Brest,* subject and object become one—multiplicity vanishes—after the committing of a murder and after the hiding of stolen gems. Quarrel then reaches his goal. He has experienced—momentarily only—wholeness and harmony within his being.

A Modern Restatement of an Old Myth

Genet has taken his own anxieties, both spiritual and sexual, described via his characters, out of the individual framework of his personal life and has turned them into a modern restatement of the old myth of sin, guilt, sacrifice, and resurrection. One man's drama in *Quarrel of Brest* has symbolically become Everyman's drama, for as Genet wrote, the author's role is "to point out the universal in a specific phenomenon" (*Q*, 333).

Quarrel is a criminal. Symbolically speaking, Genet looks on a crime as a creative act and on a criminal as a man capable of committing a creative act. The accomplishment of such an act, a traumatic experience, brings about a change of attitude and a new way of looking at things. Quarrel is just such a man. In addition to these traits, we learn, as the narrative progresses, that he possesses both human and inhuman qualities. He is a person who lives beyond the moral codes set up by man. In him are contained a composite of opposites: the criminal and the penitent, the judge and the judged, the sadist and the masochist, the redeemer and the redeemed.

Genet calls Quarrel the "angel of solitude," both spirit and flesh, material and nonmaterial, conscious and unconscious, concrete and abstract. He is as huge as the world. His feet are pillars of fire, which both nourish and destroy like the sun. He stands on water since he is a sailor; and he stands on land because the events of the narrative take place in Brest. Gliding on land as well as on water, he possesses the world and advances around his cosmos. Quarrel is the perfect nonexistent being, and is thus free from the world's justice.

The sea from which Quarrel has arrived symbolizes freedom with all of its dangers, its cross-currents, and its tides. It also represents the forces of the unconscious. To the individual struggling for identification, the sea is a nameless, universal, eternal, and infinite realm. It belongs to the collective. It is hostile to the individual who is desperately trying to find himself. The ship stands for an institution or man's conscious attitude. The wood shell of the ship represents the masks each human being wears and behind which he hides for refuge and comfort. The ship "Avenger" has docked at Brest and its cargo, namely, Quarrel, leaves it to live out his drama on land.

Each time Quarrel murders or steals (taken symbolically it means to act creatively, taken moralistically, it means to sin), he feels enriched, Genet wrote. He is eating of the book of life and thereby adding to his growth. Yet, after a while, Genet remarks, these acts deposited a kind of "dirt within him." The bitter taste of solitude or of deflation after the first flush of activity makes itself felt. Another act, more meaningful to him, now has to be perpetrated to replace the bitter with the sweet taste of accomplishment.

In general, before Quarrel *acts,* either physically or spiritually, his personality undergoes a transformation (*Q,* 209). He becomes hard, courageous, indifferent. Just before he murders Vic, he feels as though he has been infused with divine spirit. After he and Vic have smuggled the opium past customs, they both walk into the woods, as far as the former residence of Anne of Brittany. They enter a deserted court. There Quarrel feels as though he is stepping into some magic realm amid "trees stripped by the fog, thorns, and dead grass" (*Q,* 208). Suddenly, his whole body quivers. He experiences the "presence of Murder." And he knows that soon he will commit his "sacred act" (*Q,* 209). He sees himself making the sign of the cross. Then he strangles Vic. After his victim falls to the ground, he takes out his knife and cuts his carotid artery.

What is the nature of Quarrel's crime? What, symbolically speaking, has Quarrel killed when he murdered Vic? Since Vic, who represents an element of society, has helped Quarrel smuggle opium through customs, Quarrel is killing that helping element within society. (Harcamone, for example, had murdered the guard who had shown him kindness in prison.) The man of action (or the criminal) wants neither society's help nor pity. He rejects society. He wants solitude, and yet he insists on being punished for his acts. This ambivalent attitude as expressed throughout the narrative by Quarrel is Genet's own: a hatred for society and a longing to be part of it. Genet forced isolation upon himself and sacrificed those kind and warm elements within himself which might have lured him toward others, in order to bolster his own rigid defense.

The emotional upheavals Quarrel experiences by committing his crime permit him to undergo a numinous or mystical experience, the beginning of his symbolic drama of sin, guilt, sacrifice, and resurrection. After Quarrel has murdered Vic, he walks on under the trees. He stops. He is seized by a "metaphysical chill," Genet wrote. He is having a vision. He is being "visited." An "annunciation" has occurred. Now Quarrel knows that he will have to sacrifice himself to pay for his crime. Suddenly, he sees a courtroom. A trial is in process, his own. He sees his mirrored opposite. Images flash back and forth from the courtroom to the forest, which now looks like a "wonderland of marvels"; back to the courtroom; to the forest which has become "angry" and filled with thickets, thorns, and underbrush; and to the courtroom that reflects the mood of the forest. Then Quarrel hears a voice: "We demand this man's head! Blood calls for blood!" (*Q,* 213–24).

Quarrel has transcended the rational world. He has blotted out all thought. Only a single point of consciousness remains. Quarrel has become object and subject at once. He feels like a sovereign commanding his double to act and react in certain ways, either in a frightened or confident manner. He is a single unit commanding two presences: judge and judged, redeemer and redeemed. Quarrel shudders. He will carry out his sentence and expiate his crime. "I must execute myself . . ." (*Q,* 214). Quarrel says.

Quarrel knows, since he is a criminal, that is, a man of action, he has committed a deed of great import to himself. His criminal action (considered a sin in moral terms) required decisive judgment and audacity. Some criminals experience psychological ineffectiveness (considered guilt in moral terms) as an aftermath of their act. Such anxieties as guilt (moral terminology) or ineffectiveness (psychological terminology) can be assuaged or obliterated through sacrifice, the greatest being that of the self. With sacrifice there occurs an unconscious transformation from one attitude toward another, that is, a liberation of the feeling of inefficacy.

The idea of sacrifice or of expiation dates far back into mankind's history and can be seen in the ritual slaying of kings when a crop failure occurred. Such crop failure indicates impotence on the part of the ruler. The kings then were guilty of having acted ineffectively and so had to be sacrificed. In some societies the king was killed in order to improve mankind's position. Christ was sacrificed for the same reason—the salvation of man.[6] The transformation process that occurs through sacrifice is similar to an initiation ritual that permits the initiate to pass from one stage of life to another.

Sacrifice, to a great extent, is a way of self-destruction. Masochistic ways of punishment make it possible in certain cases for the person experiencing torture, either real or symbolic, to reach a new state of awareness or to be reborn psychologically. Sacrifice, then, is a stripping away or a liberation of the old attitude. Death, which is the supreme form of sacrifice, serves to wash away the sin of the individual. "And to wash oneself as well," Genet states, "that nothing remains of oneself.

And to be reborn. In order to be reborn, to die" (*Q*, 217). When in turn this newborn attitude becomes unproductive, when bitterness sets into the stomach, a similar drama is then reenacted: sin (act), guilt (feeling of ineffectiveness), sacrifice (liberation through destruction of old attitude), resurrection (birth of new attitude)—Life's eternal cycle.

The expiation that Quarrel forces upon himself after his crime is an indispensable means of leading him to his destiny and eventual transformation and liberation. Unlike Prometheus or Adam, who were punished by God, Quarrel takes matters into his own hands. He will pay for his crime by giving himself to Nono, Mme Lysiane's husband, thereby sacrificing his manliness. Such degradation as is involved in performing a homosexual act will remove the guilt (feeling of ineffectiveness) he feels as the aftermath of his sin (act—or murder). Quarrel now tastes the bitter, the aftermath of his act that he refers to as a "badly digested body." Such a sour taste can be transformed into the sweet-tasting through sacrifice. Nono then will be the instrument by which Quarrel will know expiation and regeneration. Nono must be aware of the profundity of his act because he goes about his work, Genet writes, as though it is an important religious ritual.

The question now arises as to whether Quarrel feels guilty after killing Vic? Is he driven to sacrifice? Or is he carrying out a sacrificial act devoid of all meaning? If Quarrel's guilt is experienced, the question arises as to the sincerity of his sacrifice. Is a homosexual act a sacrifice or a goal in his case? Homosexuality is a goal to the invert. To the heterosexual it is a sacrifice. There are no fixed rules for sacrifice any more than there are absolutes for good and evil. To the man suffering from a suicide fixation, death seems ultimate happiness. To the man who enjoys life, death is no joy. Quarrel's homosexual act is perhaps a culmination of all his other acts, a final step in liberating himself from society's stranglehold over him or from the constricting force of his own emotions. Genet achieves his purpose in *Quarrel of Brest*. He leaves the reader floundering around in a pool of ambiguities.

But we learn more about Quarrel as the book proceeds. Before returning to his ship, Quarrel experiences a second "visitation." He is in a forest seeking a hiding place for jewels he has stolen. He dislodges a stone in a stone wall in order to insert the jewels into the hole. As he begins working, however, he becomes hypnotized by the small stone he is dislodging. His whole being is gripped by a type of slumber, a kind of forgetfulness of self. He experiences an incorporation or incarnation into something else. He sees himself entering into the wall. His ten fingers have eyes at the tips. Quarrel has become the wall, and his individual parts are living stones.

Quarrel has experienced complete obliteration of multiplicity. He has become detached from his own being and in such a state is capable of transformation. Both creator and created, he knows at that moment that he will be saved. He has understood, penetrated into still deeper regions without and within himself, into another world beyond his own. He shudders and continues his walk. As he passes the now-abandoned prison in which so many convicts have been tortured, he looks into the small, icy rooms that still contain the iron rings and chains that had served to enslave man. And from the courtyard of the prison he visualizes a scene that, no doubt, had taken place years and years back. He sees enchained convicts, like Plato's men in the cave, shivering on cold mornings, as they look out, far into the sea, to freedom and to life.

Quarrel's acts (murder and theft), Genet wrote, had to be "sanctified." Since his second "visitation" Quarrel knows he will be saved, but he knows that someone else will have to be sacrificed. His friend Gil, also a murderer and a thief, and with whom he feels a mystical link, will be the chosen one. Quarrel feels that, like Christ, who sacrificed himself to redeem mankind, so Gil will sacrifice himself to redeem him. Quarrel's motivations are twofold: his inclinations toward mysticism and his more practical reason for self-preservation. Gil, who is accused of Théo's murder, will also be accused of Vic's murder, thereby freeing Quarrel from suspicion.

After Quarrel betrays Gil to the police, he undergoes extreme pain. He feels as if the jewels he has stolen and buried have been encrusted into his flesh. He is experiencing the "stigmata" or union with the divine. What makes the pain even more acute is that Gil, like Christ, the sacrificed one, has divined Quarrel's or Judas' betrayal. He is willing to accept his own immolation. Gil is the Christ figure and, as Genet wrote, describing a painting applicable to Gil's state of mind, "In his look and in his smile one already noticed the sadness and the despair of the Crucifixion" (*Q*, 333).

One may well ask whether Genet is mocking the ritual of sacrifice? Whether Gil's sacrifice is necessary? Whether Gil really wants to die and whether Quarrel will be redeemed? Again, Genet entices the reader to find his own answers: to discover what sacrifice means to each individual.

If sacrifice, no matter how perverse a form it takes, brings about an alteration of attitude (growth within the individual), it is associated with the sacrificial myth. Each sacrificial act has both positive and negative aspects. Adam's desire to know, for example, led him to taste the apple, which was a positive act, though negative, in that he was going against God's authority. In this sense Adam was a criminal and had to be punished. The loss of Paradise was his sacrifice. Prometheus disobeyed God's commandments in order to give man fire (knowledge). He acted for man and against Zeus in making this gift, and was punished. Christ acted against the existing order of things, which was negative, but he paved the way for the emergence of new ideas, which was positive. He sacrificed his life to reach his ends.

Quarrel's sacrifice led to his resurrection, which we interpret here as the birth of a new attitude and inner growth. He gained, as a result, the insight and the strength necessary to accept himself *in toto,* with all of his characteristics, whether they be judged morally good or evil. Consequently, Quarrel was no longer smothered by his entangling environment, nor divided by his various selves. He could look at each facet of his personality, at each individual who played a part in his life, with the cold and incisive eye of the uninvolved individual. In this respect, Quarrel had become self-sufficient, master of his destiny and of his emotions.

Just as Quarrel had lived through the great myth of sin, sacrifice, and resurrection on a personal level, from which his new attitude emerged, this drama can also be looked upon as a literary transposition of a change incurred by the author. With Genet's growing confidence as an artist, his detachment vis-à-vis his earlier environment, already noted in his works, he is better able to relate to men as a whole and to women, though still only the prostitute in them.

The Bordello

Until now the reader only glimpsed at female personalities in Genet's narratives, namely, the son killer and naive young girl. In *Quarrel of Brest* Genet introduces a new theme into his narrative, that of prostitution, one that will assume more and more importance as his literary ventures progress.

Genet's desire to degrade women has now found its perfect vehicle in the prostitute. The prostitute not only unconsciously chastises and degrades herself each time she renders a service, but the man who comes to her unconsciously experiences the same feelings. She is an object for him and not a subject. And the man is an object for her and not a subject. As such, she is dual as is he, and neither aspect of herself or of his self is related to the other. Genet projects himself on the prostitute because they both suffer from acute dualism and they both feel compelled to be humiliated.

The bordello theme in *Quarrel of Brest* replaces, to a great extent, the cathedral image prominent in *Our Lady of the Flowers* and in *Miracle of the Rose.* Symbolically speaking, Mass will said in the bordello, communion will be taken, and confession will be heard. Male priests will be transformed into female prostitutes. Indeed, one character in *Quarrel of Brest* will say on his way to Mme Lysiane's bordello, "I am going to *mass* in the Chapel on rue du Sac" (*Q,* 321).

La Féria, the bordello run by Mme Lysiane and her husband Nono, is a "solemn," "mysterious," and "fabulous" place decorated in gold and purple tones. Sailors secretly dream of this house of illusion with its warm luxury, its breasts, hips, crystals, mirrors, and perfumed champagne. When their boats approach port, they see La Féria's lantern and closed shutters and their emotions heighten. A marvelous door adds to the mystery and excitement of this magic-world:

> It was a thick panel covered over by iron, armed with long shiny metal points—perhaps of steel—pointed toward the street. For the docker or port worker the door was the sign of cruelty accompanying the rites of love. If it were a guardian, this door must have been protecting a treasure such that only insensitive dragons or invisible spirits could cross it without bleeding from the thorns—unless it opened by itself with a word or a gesture from you, docker or soldier who are tonight the happy and very pure princes penetrating via magic into forbidden domains. To be so well guarded, the treasure had to have been dangerous for the rest of the world, or of such a fragile nature, that the same type of protection was required of it as one grants to virgins (*Q,* 187).

The forty-five-year-old Mme Lysiane is happy, Genet declares. A "noble, haughty, superb" woman, she is master of herself at all moments. Such complete control has taken her years to acquire. Mme Lysiane lives in slow motion as if in a "feudal castle." She is protected from the outside world and its sun and stars and feeds "on her own sun, stars, games, and dreams. . . ." Mme Lysiane is the symbol of sumptuousness. She is magnificent not only because of her accouterments but because she remains aloof—an enigma.

Mme Lysiane's enigmatic nature stems from the fact that she is both male and female, for she has a female body and a male personality. Strong, sturdy, audacious, she is the feminine counterpart of the masculine, virile, criminal-hero type. Like other Genet heroes, Mme Lysiane is not human. She is unreal, and even the mirrors in her bordello do not reflect her image. A composite of illusions as is her house, she is what each being wants her to be. She is, in a sense, a mythlike creature.

La Féria is popular because the men who frequent it seek and find illusions there. Unconsciously, they are driven to degrade themselves and in so doing, to expiate their guilt. An undeniable sense of deficiency underlies each of Genet's heroes. By practicing humiliation, self-abnegation (which is symbolically identical with sacrifice), dismemberment, and castration,[7] they think they will liberate themselves from all the anxieties that engulf them; they go through the usual stages of sin, guilt, and sacrifice, *ad infinitum*.

Within the walls of La Féria, Genet's characters, he intimates, "ascend" through degradation. Mme Lysiane represents the Great Mother archetype in her most shameless aspects. She is like Baal and Astarte. She has no real or profound relationships with men and is present in her bordello only to exploit them. Mme Lysiane and her "vestal virgins" provide men with the seductive image they want, but in the process of capturing this image man is unmanned and degraded. He has no real feeling for any of the women in the bordello and experiences only the effect they have upon him. The same is true for the women. All live under one illusion or another.

Even Mme Lysiane has illusions. When Quarrel becomes her lover, she really wants him to possess her. Actually, he is using her for his own purposes: first, to seek revenge upon Nono for the humiliation he has forced upon himself as an act of penance after he has murdered Vic, and so decides to have relations with his "executioner's" wife; second, he would be making Mario jealous; third, in both cases he heightens his own sexual excitement by punishing himself and having relations with a woman he did not even care about; fourth, he would be proving to his brother, Robert, that he is bisexual and not only homosexual.

The situation becomes even more complicated when one considers the fact that La Féria might be a male brothel, the vestal virgins, men impersonating women; Mme Lysiane actually Monsieur. In that case, Quarrel becomes the active male homosexual intent upon making both Nono and Mario jealous. Quarrel can also be using Mme Lysiane as a foil to prove his sexual superiority over his brother. Such ambiguities as to Mme Lysiane's identity or that of any other character in the book arise as a result of Genet's own confusion on the subject.

During the entire narrative Robert has had a passive relationship with Mme Lysiane. When, however, she feels she wants to really prove her devotion to him, she sacrifices her active position and becomes a passive partner. Such "stripping" means that she will have to lift the "veil" that protects her from the outside world. In many respects this would be similar to an initiation rite. Removing her symbolic veil would mean the sacrifice of her modesty at forty-five years of age. Initiation has its dangers, and by lifting her mask she runs the risk of losing her mystery and her stature. Robert will no longer be interested in her. She will, in effect, be murdering the image Robert has of her. Such action on her part would be tantamount to self-destruction: "Reduce it to zero, destroy this moral armature which made her what she was and conferred her authority upon her" (*Q,* 295).

Mme Lysiane's sacrifice is complete. She fellates Robert. His attitude changes immediately. He looks at her with indifference. His illusions have vanished. But what are Mme Lysiane's reactions? "Vanquished, having indulged in the basest of work, she felt a feeling of great relief return to her a more certain, truer, and essential life" (*Q,* 295). In the final analysis, such veil lifting has required enormous courage, and it brings its rewards in the discovery of a more meaningful life.

But Genet, in contrast to Mme Lysiane, did not like to see a woman plain—either symbolically or realistically—that is, during her daily activities. He voiced his enthusiasm for the veil and the djellaba when he was in Morocco: "*Woman has always been a mystery for man.* It's the fact that she's hidden that makes men curious about her. Is she beautiful or not?"[8]

Mme Lysiane, unlike the flesh and blood beings Genet met during his trips in North Africa, has discovered through her sacrifice that it takes great strength to face oneself unveiled: to live life not as an image or an idol, but as a real flesh-and-blood human being, accepting oneself as one is. And for the first time, Mme Lysiane admits, "She felt her solitude and her age."[9]

Genet, too, had reached a point in his life when he was going to experience, on a literary plane, what he expressed through Quarrel's and Mme Lysiane's symbolic death and resurrection. Genet was to abandon the narrative form (with a few exceptions, notably, *The Thief's Journal*) and expend his energies in the domain of the theater. Sufficiently shorn and detached from the personal anxieties that had once held him captive, Genet could view the creatures that now emerged from within him from a distance—on stage. On an impersonal basis, then, he was sacrificing his old attitude of solitude and rejection and returning to society in the manner he saw fit. The beings he would now infuse with life would be donned in collective and inhuman characteristics, making for a mythlike drama in which universal and eternal truths are expressed.

Part Two

The Theater: From the Personal to the Collective

The time is come to set the treasure free.
To smite the locks I take the Herald's rod.
They spring apart! From brazen cauldrons, see
The flow comes welling up like golden blood.
The wealth of crowns and rings and chains comes pouring
In molten blaze that threatens their devouring.

—Goethe, *Faust,* part 2

Chapter Six
A Theater of Symbols

> The mind is its own place, and in itself
> Can make a heaven of hell, a hell of heaven.
> —Milton, *Paradise Lost*

Genet's plays are to his novels what symphonies are to string quartets—the quintessence of his art. His theater is a thoughtful and mature reappraisal of the basic themes that run through his ebullient and youthful narrative works: illusion and reality, life and death, good and evil, strong and weak, old and young, ephemeral and eternal, collective and individual, conscious and unconscious.[1]

Genet's theater is hedonistic and devoid of a moral purpose. It sets no ideal. As Roger Blin declared: "His theater is an expression of himself in that it is constantly renewing itself, continually offering new series and stages of revolt."[2]

Audiences present at a Genet production witness a religious ritual. Genet sees God in whatever he does. His plays, therefore, are sacred dramas during the course of which the deepest parts of man are moved communally through the common sharing of the theatrical ceremony.

The play replaced theft in Genet's life. For Genet the act of stealing has always been infused with God's presence. It is something serious and not to be taken lightly. In the past, he created and followed a ritual before committing a theft. First, he used to offer up his miseries to God. He even dedicated his crime to God. Then he performed a deed that he thought might be pleasing to the gods within the objects he had set out to rob. So he gave money to the poor, or helped the blind across the street, and so forth.

As the years passed, theft no longer seemed to satisfy him. His creative energy required something less negative, more engrossing. Genet felt, unconsciously, that he was being stunted by his criminal life. He needed an outlet in which he could find fulfillment and in which there was room for development. Narrative writing was the answer. But this form of expression was short-lived. After pouring forth his hates and lusts, developing his philosophy of life through poetized song, Genet became more reflective and subdued. The mature artist who had evolved his own disciplines, the aesthetician whose eyes pierced through the walls of appearances, emerged. The theater would now be his vehicle. It would be called his crime because the theater as conceived by Genet was an audacious, aggressive, and mystical act—brought out into the open before adversaries—the audience. All present and witnessing Genet's crime (the play) would become associated with it and involved in it as a living mystery.

What is seen on stage during a Genet theatrical performance does not resemble "the visible world" as audiences think of it. Genet's theater is a theater of symbols by means of which the imagination and sensibilities of each person in the audience becomes activated: "One can only dream of an art that would be a profound web of active symbols of speaking to the audience in a language in which nothing is said but everything is portended."[3] Once the imagination in man has been moved, secret affinities and relationships appear among the characters who are really metaphors, acting and reacting on the stage: "I hope thereby to do away with characters—which stand up, usually only by virtue of psychological convention—to the advantage of signs as remote as possible from what they are meant first to signify, though nevertheless attached to them in order, by this sole link, to unite the author with the spectator, in short, so to contrive that the characters on the stage would be only metaphors of what they are supposed to represent."[4] The Mass, Genet wrote, serves as the supreme metaphor, the ceremony and dramatic performance at its highest perfection.

On a stage not unlike our own, on a platform, the problem was to reconstitute the end of a meal. On the basis of this one particular which is now barely perceptible in it, the loftiest modern drama has been expressed daily for two thousand years in the sacrifice of the Mass. The point of departure disappears beneath the profusion of ornaments and symbols that still overwhelm us. Beneath the most familiar of appearances—a crust of bread—a god is devoured. I know nothing more theatrically effective than the elevation of the host: when finally this appearance appears before us—but in what form, since all heads are bowed, the priest along knows; perhaps it is God himself or a simple white pellet that he holds at the tip of his four fingers—or that other moment in the Mass when the priest, having broken the host on the paten in order to show it to the faithful puts it together again and eats it. The host crackles in the priest's mouth! A performance that does not act upon my soul is vain. It is vain if I do not believe in what I see, which will end—which will never have been when the curtain goes down.[5]

The theater, then, is no frivolous game for Genet. It is not a "diversion," in modern theatrical language. A numinous experience is lived through during a theatrical ceremony. The participants, as in Greek theater or in the Mass, are communally drenched in the divine and then transformed. The mortal individual attending his theater becomes during the performance an immortal and collective power. The ephemeral in man spins out into the eternal.

Paradoxically, once the theatrical spell has been cast and communion has taken place between author, actor, and spectator—it must be shattered. Such a rupture serves to increase the tension in the theater. And though the author wants everyone to believe in what he is saying, audience credibility must be destroyed through shock: by insults and attacks leveled at an audience; by an actor as he winks his eyes; by lighting effects; by pornography, by strange or haunting rhythms in speech, gesture, and gait; by the actor's declamatory tone; and so forth. In being destroyed, the theatrical magic becomes that much more extreme and the communion experience more intense.

The actors performing in symbolic and metaphoric plays, in which what is not spoken is of more importance than what is, must be of very special quality. Actors must resemble shadow-play beings. They must be facades or screens, an example of a world of appearances masking an inner reality. As the play unfolds, their outer coverings must be burned off so that the living core of man gestures its way across the stage through the actor. The actor then is both Creator and Incarnator. He is a "sign charged with signs." He is a paradox, at once real and unreal, concrete and abstract, one and multiple.

To train an actor for this special task, to be the visible manifestation of inner contents, one should establish not "conservatories" but "seminaries." The actor on stage then could become what the priest is during a Mass, a "forest of symbols," to use Baudelaire's terms. He would reveal to the audience or parishioners, as the case may be, reflections of their own images, smudged perhaps, but recognizable. As communion begins and takes hold of the faithful in the theater or in the cathedral, they plunge into a deeper reality, reach back into centuries, into man's heritage where beings existed in their totality. There the spectators dwell in their depths and return to the roots and sources of all mankind.

Audiences are frequently alarmed when confronted with Genet's visions of swirling and disturbing images—a world each spectator knows really exists. They are disarmed, frequently, by Genet's ability to evoke laughter, they are provoked, angered, and bludgeoned a moment later with renewed vigor. The spectator is seduced at other times by the haunting rhythms, the "sheer beauty and poetry of Genet's language" or is caught up and shaken by the mirror images and paradoxes forever present. Genet's theater is one of willed multiplicity where the individual spectator, who desperately tries to find himself amid galleries of images and reflections, is forever caught up by a splintered image of himself, imprisoned in a series of "reflections of reflections." Roger Blin stated the following concerning Genet's ambiguity: "But these 'reflections of reflections' present in Genet's plays are limitless, and even the author himself gets lost in this labyrinth. For those who can see, many paths and chambers have been opened in this endless hall of mirrors by the text and the actors' interpretation of this text. There comes a point, however, when the actor becomes impotent, unable to correct what Genet himself failed to clarify."[6]

Genet illustrates in five short and sparkling narrative works certain points inherent in his theater: willed multiplicity and facelessness, in his ballet *'Adame Miroir;* the drama as a passage from the individual to the collective, in "Le Funambule" (The Tightrope Walker); reality and illusion in a timeless and spaceless world, in "L'Atelier d'Albert Giacometti" (The workshop of Alberto Giacometti); a meditation on time feeding on its own continuum, in "L'Etrange Mot D' . . ." (The strange word D . . .'); and the emotional reactions of a viewer and the object being viewed in "Ce qui est resté d'un Rembrandt déchiré en petits carrés" (What Remained of a Rembrandt torn into very regular small squares and thrown into the toilet).

Willed Multiplicity: Facelessness

In *'Adame Miroir* (1949) Genet has transported his personal drama of inner multiplicity and facelessness to the stage. Even the title of this work is ambiguous. The deformation of the words *Adam* and *Madame* rob them of their identities: for *Adam* becomes *Adame* and *Madame* loses its first letter. Both words are at once male and female or neither one nor the other.

The idea for the ballet *'Adame Miroir* came to Genet at a fairground in Montmartre known as the Palace of Mirrors. Genet described this labyrinthine structure in *The Thief's Journal.* It was partitioned with "plates of glass, some silvered and some transparent" (*TJ,* 265). The idler visiting the fair paid and then entered the Palace of Mirrors. Genet continued: "the problem is to get out. You move about desperately, bumping into your own image or into a visitor cut off from you by a glass. The onlookers witness from the street the search for the invisible path" (*TJ,* 264). Genet recalled a similar scene he had witnessed in Antwerp. Both memories of the men imprisoned in their own reflections troubled him, and so he set them together in ballet form.

'Adame Miroir[7] takes place in a palace. The walls of the corridors are covered with mirrors, and the ceilings are heavy with chandeliers. A young and handsome Sailor dressed in white dances before a mirror in which he sees his Image. He turns around and sees another reflection of himself in another mirror. He becomes frightened and the greater his anguish, the more frenetic is his dancing. He notices, however, that the motions of the Image he sees in the mirror do not correspond exactly to his own. The Sailor and his Image begin dancing together. But when the Image tries to approach the Sailor, the latter runs away. Death, in the form of Domino, enters and separates the Sailor from his Image. Domino pursues the Sailor, stabs him with the stem of his fan, and drags him off the stage. The Image watches the scene unmoved. Domino reenters and begins to pursue the Image. He catches him. They exchange costumes. Now the ex-Domino reveals himself to be the Sailor of before. The new Domino who was the Image pursues the Sailor who flees into a mirror. The ex-Domino wants to follow him but cannot and bumps against his own reflection. Astonished, he moves back and so does his reflection. He looks about and sees the Sailor's beret on the floor, the only material proof of the action having taken place. He walks off the stage as each mirror casts back the Image of a Domino just like him.

Not only is there extreme diversity and ambiguity in *'Adame Miroir,* but the characters are all faceless. They are never themselves because they have no identities. They are forever being transformed into something else. Yet these same beings are prisoners of their own lacunae, that is, their valueless, formless, and amorphous existences. They are constantly deceived. Everything in their world is elusive. Only Matter, in the form of the Sailor's beret, vouches for the actuality of the action. But this too is a lie, because nothing is tangible, as nothing is stationary, and perhaps even the beret was imagined. Man, a prison of Matter and of his own limitations in the Platonic sense of the world, bases his reality and existence on Matter, which is as deceptive or perhaps more so than anything else, because it gives one a false sense of reality and security. To strip and rid the world of Matter and of exteriors, to penetrate within this world of mirrors and facades, is to render the incomprehensible comprehensible—to discover self.

From the Individual to the Collective

Since the theater is a sacred ceremony, the spectator immerses himself in the drama on stage just as the parishioner takes communion in church. In so doing, he renounces his individual existence and becomes part of the collective body. The emotional upheaval that takes place during such a passage within the soul of the performing artist and the spectator is explained in Genet's dazzling narrative piece, *The Tightrope Walker* (1958). Dedicated to his lover, Abdallah, a young tightrope artist, Genet's prose describes in concise terms both the tightrope walker's stunt and his own reactions to it.

Like the criminal and the actor, the tightrope walker must have sufficient audacity and courage to vanquish death. Tightrope walking is a cruel art, Genet explains, as cruel as the *corrida* (bullfight), poetry, war, and the theater. It requires extreme exactitude on the part of the performer; the least error leads to his sudden death.

Solitude is also a common denominator between the tightrope walker and the actor; the writer and the sculptor. L. A. C. Dobrez wrote, "The tightrope walker is his own work of art, escaping himself and seeking himself . . . and always within this mortal and bleached solitude."[8] Their solitude will be brought to light by their art, which is the physical manifestation of their most secret selves and is the only means of communicating with the outside world. As they reach out to man through their creations, they become part of the collective being. "Let your solitude," Genet wrote, "paradoxically be in full light, and obscurity be composed of the thousands of eyes which judge you."[9]

Solitude, inviting the profoundest of "wounds," is a factor involved in encouraging the artist to reach deeply into the most hidden spheres of being. Solitude, though excoriating, must be cultivated, as must sorrow. For only then may the work of art be fashioned: "I wonder where resides . . . the secret wound in which every man seeks refuge when his pride is threatened, when he is wounded. It's this wound . . . which is going to swell, magnify. Every man knows how to enter it, to the point of becoming the wound itself, a kind of secret and suffering heart" (*F,* 188).

Genet juxtaposes scorching fire images, viewed as purifying agents, with icy ones, eliciting their opposites, conditions of stasis, to reveal the moat that cuts off each individual from his neighbor on all external scores. White, a symbol for the complete artist because it is a composite of all colors of the spectrum, has now been brushed on Genet's canvas. The tightrope walker slowly becomes transformed into a block of ice. He has "frozen over," just as an actor does when a performance begins. "As these waves rise—like the cold beginning at Socrates' feet, penetrating his legs, thighs, belly—their coldness seizes your heart and freezes it" (*F,* 188).

As ice, the artist has become insensitive to his audience. The disparate parts of his being have been fused in an extreme tension of will. Yet, Genet goes on, "in your center a hearth never ceased to feed this glacial death which entered through your feet (*F,* 188). This "hearth," or ball of fire within the artist symbolizes the creative energy that incites him toward greatness, that nourishes him, but only in one area (his art), while withdrawing food from other parts of his body and psyche and leaving them frozen and paralyzed. If the artist were to remain in this state for long periods of time, he would be destroyed, either by fire (his inner creative force) or by ice (rigid unproductivity).

The artist is like Narcissus, Genet declares: a "solitary lover pursuing his own image," that is, his identity and original unity. In his quest, however, he feels the "nostalgia, joy, gratitude and mortal solitude" of the instrument with which he works—the rope in the tightrope walker's case and the play in the actor's. He discovers the rope's core, its "secret possibilities," and infuses life into it just as the actor breathes life into his creations. Before the act, the rope was "dead, mute, blind" as the actor's script (*F,* 175). While being danced on, the rope lives and speaks. It is loved carnally by the performer, and at night, when returning it to its box, the artist-actor rubs his cheek against the rope as a sign of gratitude. The rope has become a phallic symbol, a fructifier that injects life into the artist. The rapport between the actor and his decors and costumes is similar. The rope is personified by Genet. The rope becomes a panther seeking blood. As such, it must be constantly tamed. Similarly, a play requires the blood of actors and must forever be mastered. Man's instincts (the animal), in other words, must be channeled in order to become fruitful; otherwise they are destructive forces: the struggle, then, is never ending between the physical and spiritual: the rope and the performer, the actor and his play.

The tightrope walker as well as the actor has become "as pale as death." His pallor, however, is not born of fear. It comes about as his "hearth" of inner fire withdraws from his body and goes outside of it. In a series of glowing images, Genet describes how this inner fire inundates the entire arena. His energies have been released and have joined the collective—therefore, he is left pale. The "hearth" that had been imprisoned within his body has now broken through. The tightrope walker is empty as he stands high above the crowd, muscles flexed, pirouetting, hopping, his taut body seized by his art. Audiences are now looking at a "dead man," an "apparition," an image, a performer divested of his innards, obliterated of soul and psyche. Only then will the dancer have reached perfection. The individual artist, inhabited by art alone, has earned his "transparency"; pure luminosity now shines through him. Like Divinity, so the artist dies to the world in order to assume a higher dimension of being. Only then is the personal act transformed into a collective experience.

Reality and Illusion in a Timeless and Spaceless World

In *The Workshop of Giacometti* (1958), Genet tried to capture and hold the inner man. He wanted to know man as he is and as he had been centuries ago. It was this all-time being, the primitive in man, before life's superimposed reality caked itself upon him, that Genet tried to seize. He had to hack off the centuries of grime that covered man's soul: in other words, to bring the dead back to life. This, too, was the actor's task when confronted with the written play—to give dead words life.

In dealing with death and life, Genet found inspiration in Giacometti's poignant statues. In what is one of the most extraordinary art criticisms ever written—on a par with Baudelaire's *Salons*—Genet describes in *The Workshop of Giacometti* how, fascinated and terrified, he was drawn to the works of this artist and how they helped him walk through time and space. Genet had experienced similar feelings, he wrote in this essay, in the Louvre Museum, the day he first saw an ancient statue of the dying and resurgent god Osiris, who as king of the underworld weighed and balanced the souls of the dead.

Genet was drawn to Giacometti's sculptures by their strength, weight, power, and dimension. When he saw Giacometti's portrait of him, he was in awe: an elongated head, tense, taut, stretched upward into empty space filled him with virtual disbelief. Giacometti had revealed suffering, the constrictions of closure, and, at the same time, the passionate desire for open air. Like a bird in flight, the head strained to move ever beyond the visible empirical domain, into its own transparency. Absence had become visible; concretion had taken on dimension; silence had become lyrified.

As for the other Giacometti heads, figures, and torsoes, Genet was moved by their sensuality; as he slid his hand up and down the bronze sculptures, he felt living beings palpitating beneath their surfaces. He found visually appealing the broken and elongated lines issuing from a blocklike pedestal that encased the feet of a statue, while the rest of it shot up into space, thinning out in flight to end in a "minuscule head." He admired the "diamondlike" quality of Giacometti's vision: it had allowed him to infuse life into his creations; it had encouraged him to cast shadows and reflections on the white page or on the sculpted form, thereby heightened the brilliance of his works, inviting light, space, and shadow to circulate freely. Giacometti, who had infused life into his creations, Genet noted, never allowed his own personality to intrude, but permitted the statues and drawings to live a life of their own. Similarly, the actor, too, must create a character and himself withdraw from it.

Genet had discovered in Giacometti's sculptures what the actor must discern in a play; a secret and solitary world peopled with the dead come back to life. Space and time have been abolished: communion between the living (the artist and the actor) and the dead (statues as objects) has taken place on one of the most profound and secret levels known to man, a level inaccessible to conscious awareness, a suprapersonal, transpersonal realm that can manifest itself only through archetypal imagery (the statue—the play). Once the emotional impact of encountering this archetypal image has been felt, the artist, the actor, and the spectator have lived a numinous experience: the revelation of something extraordinary or divine within them. That is why Genet compared Giacometti's statues to gods, goddesses, and priests, and a room inhabited by such creations to a temple.

When Genet was in the presence of a Giacometti statue, he was overwhelmed by a feeling of "nostalgia." He longed for a "civilization that would try to venture beyond the measurable," where man would not be interested in the visible or material "world of appearances," but would instead "denude himself sufficiently to discover this secret place." Such a revelation could result in a change of attitude and could cause a completely different "human adventure" to be lived. Genet's discovery of the inner world, a spacelessness and timelessness, reminded him of a deformed man who had suddenly stripped himself of his clothes and had become aware, for the first time, of his deformity.

Just as Giacometti's eyes pierced through the flesh and sinews of man, chiseling them away, so the actor should proceed with his script. What should stand before viewers is the burning core, the eternal in man. Stripped of all trappings and coverings, reduced to bear essentials, the artist (the actor by extension) comes upon a whole untapped dimension within his being where he can discover the insights needed to live "a totally different human adventure." In this lonely domain, separated from all others, the creative individual finds and illuminates the beauty he has discovered, that "singular wound" in each being "into which he retreats when he wants to leave the world for temporary but profound solitude"[10] (*A*, 10).

Giacometti's statues spoke to Genet as the actor speaks to his audience. They forced open his wounds of solitude, ushering him into the timeless and spaceless world of the dead. There, when facing a face, Genet isolated it from other, animate or inanimate, objects. Only then was the burning core revealed to him in its ephemeral and eternal aspects. The person's solitude, Genet writes, or that of "the object represented which is given back to us, and we, who observe, in order to perceive it . . . must experience the space not of its continuity but discontinuity" (*A*, 20). All creation carried and does carry this same burden of loneliness, and for this reason, Genet wrote, Giacometti's statues have a look of eternity about them. They are solitary and sad, as though they had been dug out from layers of earth or baked in flaming ovens and then left to cool.

Giacometti and his statues, like the actor and his play, are a composite of opposites: both familiar and inaccessible, male and female, contemporary and ancient. They are haughty and humble, immobile and mobile. They are mute and vocal, as objects created by the artist and infused with life, and as objects in and of themselves. They speak out their solitude, which is man's solitude. They commune with the forces in the universe, recognizing "the solitude in all beings and in all objects," which seems to say: "I am alone . . . my solitude knows yours" (*A*, 57).

Time Feeding Its Own Continuum

In "The Strange word D' . . ." (1968), a seminal meditation upon theater, time, and death, Genet sets forth his ideas concerning the dramatic Event or Advent. The goal of theater, Genet intimates, is to make the spectator escape what has been labeled historical time, but is, in reality, theological time. The moment the theatrical Advent begins, time as we know it must be annihilated; categories, whether religious or political, must no longer exist. Flowing, fleeting, bounding, hopping about in complete freedom, the Advent exists outside of historical time, as if suspended in some transparent sphere and feeding on its own continuum.

Genet opposes the notions of the Christian West, which seeks to incarcerate what mystics call the eternal present and which he identifies with "dramatic time" within a linear frame that has its "origin in a hypothetical Incarnation." Is it any wonder, Genet writes, that such theater, with its limited and specific time sequences and events, interests only Westerners? Such ideations have no universal or eternal appeal. To transcend such a shortsighted view, Genet suggests that audiences be offered a multiplication of "Advents" in discontinuous and orderless sequences. Only then would the Christian era, which establishes the beginning of time with the "Very contestable Nativity," would be abolished.[11]

As for the theatrical Advent, it must not consist of just anything. It can find its "pretext" for existence in anything: an isolated but meaningful occurrence in the temporal world and presented as "fragmented" in an eternal present, feeds on its own continuum. The results may be overwhelming: the dramatic act may sear and burn the spectator with a "fire that can be extinguished only when fanned." The "verbal architecture," of the dramatic Advent, must be both "grammatical and ceremonial," born as it were, from a void, that is *chaos,* or that precreated *prima materia,* and when incarnated, reveal this same endless, dimensionless, timeless void.

As for the theater itself, even though its ideal architecture still remains to be discovered, Genet believes it should rest on a "fixed," immobilized," space, thus rendering the Advent enacted within such a structure, "responsible" for the "irreversible act" that will be viewed and judged on stage. Once the architect discovers the right shape and contours for the *temenos;* once the *real* meaning of theater is experienced, those involved in creating the Advent, must work "with an almost sacerdotal and smiling gravity."

Theaters, Genet suggests—and this too is innovative on his part—must be errected in local urban cemeteries. Like the artist who has died, vanished within his creation, or whose life has been struck down in order for the work to live, so a theatrical performance should be experienced in an unflawed or absolute atmosphere: the realm of those who are in transition. The seat of the transformatory process—from life to death or from the unborn to the born drama—would be unforgettable if set in a necropolis. Genet takes Mozart's *Don Juan* as an example. At the drama's finalé, and prior to their reentering the profane world, the spectators would walk out onto and amid the dead buried in the earth. Upon contact with that ineffable sphere of being, Don Juan's fulgurating and fulminating end would again erupt—become actuated in the souls and psyches of the spectators. The otherworldly atmosphere thus concretized would endow the just-experienced staged Advent with ceremonious and religious dignity.

Genet's cemetery—and Genet stresses this point—is not "dead," nor is it peopled with only a few steles. It is "alive," active, with new bodies being entombed daily. Going even further in his innovative concept, Genet suggests the possibility of constructing a theater on the side of a crematorium: its "stiff, oblique, and phallic chimney" creating an unforgettable stylized ritual—a vision of eternal and dimensionless proportions.

The Object and the Viewer

Genet's essay "What remained of a Rembrandt torn into very regular small squares and thrown into the toilet" (1968) was written twelve years after the author had experienced an emotional upheaval. The incident took place in a London museum while Genet was "gazing" at some of Rembrandt's finest works. Because he could never shake off the viscerality of their impact on him—the feelings that flowed between viewer and object viewed—he wondered whether something was wrong with him. How could he account, he asked, for the power of the emotions surging forth within him during those moments, and, more importantly, for their long lasting effect upon him: "What are those paintings that I can't shake off?"[12] The answer lies buried in Genet's essay on this seventeenth-century Dutch painter.

"What remained of a Rembrandt" is composed of two autonomous columns: one consisting of a commentary of the other, triggering correspondences between the two that emerge every now and then through associations, discontinuities, and deconstructions. Although the statements made in both columns are singularly different, they converge at times on an emotional plane; "flowing" into each other as the relationships between the viewer and the object being viewed and depicted grow closer, only to grow apart, then reject each other in sequences of negations, annihilations, rebirths, and dismemberments.

Derrida comments on Genet's text:

> "What Remained of a Rembrandt" develops over its two columns a theory or an event of general equivalence: of subjects—"every man *is worth* another"—of terms, of contraries exchanged without end, of the "*je m'ec* . . ." ("je m'écoulais," "I was flowing" in my body, in the body of the other). *S'écouler,* to flow: a syntagm, relayed through "*écoeurement*" (disgust), the "exchanged regard," the "feeling of *s'écouler*" (flowing), "*je m'étais écoulé*" (I had been flowing), "*j'écrivais*" (I was writing), *je m'écrivais* (I was writing myself) in "*tant d'écoeurement*" (so much disgust), so much "sadness"—(the word returns six times in fewer than ten pages), of the infinite exchange between two columns that regard themselves in reverse.
>
> X, an almost perfect chiasm(us), more than perfect, of two texts, each one set facing [*en regard*] the other: a gallery and a graphy that guard one another and disappear from view. But the pictures are written, and what (one) writes (oneself) is seen regarded by the painter.[13]

The inward trajectory—really a self-interrogation—effected in "What remained of a Rembrandt" encourages Genet once again to *face* that being within him as an individual and as an archetype, that is, as a collective power emanating from his objective psyche.

The discourse takes place in the third-class compartment of a train going from Salon to Saint-Rambert-d'Albon. The atmosphere, enclosed like a tomb/womb, encourages a meditative mood. By chance, the narrator's gaze meets that of a man in his fifties seated in the compartment. Although dirty and repulsive, it is through his *regard* (look), which "butted" against the narrator's, then "melted" into his, that he realizes that the "distress" and the "emotion" he thought he had seen in the "other" man was in fact a reflection of his own that had "butted" on the other man's "by chance and in the solitude and forgetfulness of self-oblivion."

This "revelation" comes to him as a shocking discovery. It makes him conscious of "a kind of universal identity" between all beings that transcends the reality of individuality. As he feels himself "flowing" out of his body, through his "eyes," into that other being (really his own flowing into him), he experiences the impact and motility of those elements inhabiting that collective sphere implicit in all beings.

How, Genet suggests in his essay, did the narrator intuit the notion that "every man *is identical* with every other" at this particular moment? How did this idea, which had been enunciated time and time again throughout history, surface after the meeting of a casual "look"? These questions are never really answered. No matter, the narrator experiences a semblance of fulfillment when he realizes that each person, although temporarily isolated in his individual "shell," is himself in himself, while also existing in another. Still, and strangely enough, the narrator remarks that he feels no real rapport or feelings of tenderness or affection for that *other* being outside of himself.

What did make an impact upon the narrator, was the motility and quicksand nature of life. If a thought surfaces into consciousness for no knowable reason, then nothing is certain in life, he states. There is no such thing as security or stasis. No sooner had this notion concerning the fluidity of life floated into his being than the world began to float around him and nausea overcame him; vertigo set in. There was no terra firma. That "A solid void which never ceased to perpetuate me" was the only truth, he realized, saddened him and filled him with a gnawing nostalgia.

As the reader absorbs the narrator's musings, printed on the left side of the page, he also enters into complicity with Genet's commentary on Rembrandt's later paintings, printed on the right side. When gazing at this master's paintings, one's view is "heavy, a bit bovine," Genet writes, restrained by an inexplicably "grave force." The figures, whether those depicted in *The Jewish Bride* or another of Rembrandt's canvases, are flesh embedded in matter. "However delicate her face and serious her expression," Genet knows that the Jewish bride has "an ass" and that at any moment she is capable of raising her skirts. The same may be said of Rembrandt himself in his first self-portrait: "the mass of flesh increases from one painting to the next. . . ."

However, after Rembrandt lost what he treasured most, his mother and his wife, he went through his ordeal by fire: modifying, then ridding his work of what encumbered it, freeing it of its anecdotal self. In so doing, he transformed its solitude and frenzy into eternality; its concretion into transparency; its temporality into the cosmic.

The identity of the figures depicted on a Rembrandt canvas are of no interest to Genet. Indeed, it is by this lack of knowledge or absence that mystery comes into being and emotions are aroused. The more he gazed *into* Rembrandt's canvases, "the *less the portraits referred me to anyone.*" What fascinated him, for example, were the wrinkles he recalled years later on some of the faces of Rembrandt's figures. But it could have been anyone's face, what was involved were the wrinkles that spoke to Genet and aroused feeling.

The sadness Genet sees in the faces on Rembrandt's canvases is a living reminder of "The sadness of being in the world. . . ." However, this sadness belongs to Genet, to his narrator, to the man seated in the third-class compartment in the train—to the reader of the essay.

Because Rembrandt depersonalizes his models and prunes objects, thus divesting them of any identifiable trait, his eye and his painter's palette are endowed with weight and reality. As Derrida wrote:

> The word "regard" that opens the right column fixes you again at the end of the left column. You think you are the one who regards, and it is the text of the picture (Rembrandt) that oversees and informs against you, sketches and denounces you—what? from elsewhere. "The remain(s), all the remain(s), seemed to me the effect of an optical error provoked by my appearance itself necessarily faked. Rembrandt was the first to denounce me. Rembrandt! That severe finger that brushes aside [*ecarte*] showy rags and shows . . . what? An infinite, an infernal transparency." . . Now this double theory (or double column taking note of the general equivalence of subjects or contraries) describes itself as it feigns to recount some pictures, some "*works of art,*" as the suspense of the *verily:* remain(s) beyond the true and the false, neither entirely true nor entirely false. That (*Ça*) is stretched between two subjects absolutely independent in their distress but nonetheless interlaced, interwoven, entwined like two lianas orphaned from their tree.[14]

As in theater, sham and artifice are also all-important in painting, Genet states: "And I need hardly say that Rembrandt's entire work has meaning—at least for me—only if I know that what I have just written is false."

So the artist and the actor share their wounds and solitude, their masks and deceits with the multitudes in a communion feast where the dead are resurrected by means of the metaphor; reality is resurrected with the help of illusion, the past through the present, the eternal or divine by means of the ephemeral, the collective via the individual. The theater for Genet is a paradox—a collection of symbols and shadows—mirroring a world as vital as is life.

Genet's theater is heroic and audacious. It shoots through the externals of contemporary scenic techniques and presents its audiences with man's succulent but blackened marrow.

Chapter Seven
Deathwatch

> Now the Lord had said unto Abraham, Get thee out of the country, and from thy kindred, and from thy father's house, unto a land that I will show thee.
>
> —Genesis 12:1

> Think not that I am come to send peace on earth: I came not to send peace, but a sword.
> For I am come to set a man at variance against his father, and the daughter against her mother, and the daughter-in-law against her mother-in-law.
> And man's foes shall be they of his own household.
>
> —Matthew 10:34–36

Haute Surveillance (*Deathwatch*), Genet's first play, was presented at the Théâtre des Mathurins in February 1949. The sets were designed by André Baurepair, and the play was directed by Jean Marchat with the help of the inexperienced author. Audiences, unprepared for Genet's new brand of theater and for a production stressing the play's realism instead of its dreamlike qualities, received it coldly.

Deathwatch is a classically constructed one-act play that adheres to the unities of time, place, and action. The action involves a trinity of criminals: Green Eyes, twenty-two years old, is "tall" and "very handsome"; Maurice, seventeen years old, is "small" and "pretty"; Lefranc twenty-three years old, is "tall" and "handsome." Green Eyes and Lefranc wear felt shoes and walk about noiselessly; Maurice is barefoot. The costumes are black and white. In the prison cell setting the protagonists are both observers and the observed, watching each other as the play's title *Surveillance* indicates, thus both increasing their understanding of their situation and remaining on guard against their fellow inmates.

Since, as Genet wrote, "the entire play unfolds as in a dream," the unconscious meanderings of the prisoners must also be taken into account when exploring *Deathwatch;* that is, their whole fantasy life. That the stage directions call for "as much light as possible, we are in prison," not only creates a willed ambiguity between reality and the dream, but also brings to the fore a whole metaphysical dimension. The prison cell, then, comes to represent a reality of sorts, but of a kind reminiscent of the men imprisoned in Plato's allegory of the Cave or in Sartre's *No Exit*.

The Plot

Deathwatch begins as Green Eyes tries to separate Lefranc and Maurice who are fighting and vying for his affection. Green Eyes is their hero because he murdered a prostitute in a frenzy of anger. The crime "came to him," he did not seek it out, Genet comments. Lefranc stands a rank lower in this hierarchy because he is merely a petty criminal. It is he who has been writing letters to Green Eyes's wife at Green Eyes's request. He is accused by his hero of trying to win her affections, but denies this accusation. Lefranc's goal has been to sever her relationship with Green Eyes. He wants his hero all to himself and does not want to share him with anyone. Maurice is a juvenile delinquent who idealizes his hero and would do anything, even murder, for him. Green Eyes suggests that either Lefranc or Maurice, both of whom will be released from jail shortly, murder his wife. Which one will risk his life for his hero?

The conversation centers around Snowball, a Negro who is never seen in the play but who reigns supreme, as a deity, a "king," over the entire "fortress," or prison. He is the master criminal, the authentic hero-god-criminal who murdered for gain, who faces his reality and is completely independent. Green Eyes is not on a par with Snowball because he murdered out of fury. His act was not lucidly perpetrated and so was not authentic.

Green Eyes relates his crime to his two cellmates who, until this time, have never known the details and thought his crime superior to that of Snowball. Green Eyes leaves the cell to meet his woman who is visiting, and when he returns with the guard, he accepts the two cigarettes the guard brings him—a gift from Snowball. In return, he offers his woman to the guard. After Green Eyes accepts the gift, he is never again the complete hero figure to Maurice.

Lefranc confesses to his cellmates that he is, in reality, "The Avenger," the great criminal. Maurice makes fun of him and tells him that he will never be able to join their group, that he will never be an authentic criminal and will always remain an outsider. Reacting violently to this accusation, unconsciously anxious to prove his authenticity as a criminal, Lefranc strangles Maurice as Green Eyes stands on a basin turned upside down and looks on.

But even after Lefranc has murdered Maurice, Green Eyes does not consider him an authentic criminal. Furthermore, he is disgusted with Lefranc for killing a boy: "Killed him for nothing! For the glory of it. . . . And you thought you could become, all by yourself, without the help of heaven, as great as me! . . . I didn't want what happened to me to happen. It was all given to me. A gift from God or the devil, but something I didn't want."[1] Lefranc has been acting in bad faith because, as he says, "I wanted to become what you were. . . . My misfortune comes from something deeper. It comes from myself" (*MD,* 162). Green Eyes knocks on the door to call the guard, and Lefranc confesses in the closing lines of the play, "I am alone."

Although the critic Lucien Goldmann makes short shrift of *Deathwatch,* considering Genet's poetic universe a dramatization "of the nonconformist underclass" and "a strictly coherent work," it is in fact a complex ritualistic enactment of a myth, a religious celebration, a mystification with its mystagogues and *mystai.*[2]

The Criminal-Hero: The Criminal-Hero Worshiper

Deathwatch is a religious abstraction, a dramatization of the myth of the hero and the hero worshiper. The hero's function and obligations to himself and to society are age-old. Usually, the hero struggles symbolically to overthrow "the old law," that is, the decayed and unproductive elements within society and, by extension, within himself. In the throes of this struggle, he brings forth the "new law." Heroism is a creative force that rests on an aggressive act. Such activity makes for evolution, productivity, and independence, not only in terms of the individual and his growth, but also in terms of society's maturation. This struggle waged by the hero, if successful, is the culmination of an "audacious," "courageous," or "criminal" act. (Criminal is to be taken in the broad sense of the word. The hero is a destroyer since he tries to get rid of the old established traditions.) When "the Lord said unto Abraham, Get thee out of thy country . . .[3] he meant for him to break with the old tradition. Christ's message was an extension of the same idea, but much more outspoken and violent: "Think not that I come to send peace on earth: I came not to send peace, but a sword."[4]

Deathwatch is the story not of three men (Green Eyes, Maurice, and Lefranc), but of three aspects of one man, of three shadows or parasites living off each other. None of the three men is a complete a real hero at the beginning of the play. Green Eyes, Lefranc, and Maurice want to be heroes, but instead are hero worshipers. They try to fill their feelings of emptiness by living out somebody else's existence and, in so doing, abdicate part of themselves. This abdication or destruction of certain aspects of their personalities is manifested on several different occasions throughout the play: Green Eyes's desire to give away his woman and to have her killed; Lefranc's repeated donning of Green Eyes's jacket; and Maurice's action of thrusting back his nonexistent lock of hair. These three men have never really faced themselves: they are afraid to look within. During the play they will shed their coverings: Maurice's death, Lefranc's murder of Maurice, which shocks him into accepting his solitude, and Green Eyes's final admission of his subservience to Snowball.

The names of the characters themselves in some ways serve to indicate the personalities of the bearers. The Negro, the supreme and authentic criminal, the god or true hero, is called Snowball. He combines life's opposites: black and white, evil and good, sun and moon, color and the reflection of it, conscious and unconscious forces. He is unity. He lives in higher regions, in the cell above, as Marcamone had in the *Miracle of the Rose.* He is remote and remains a mystery because he is never present on stage, is rarely seen by the three cellmates, and so the illusions of his totality and perfection can persist. He is described as being a "savage," of "eating his victims," of "shining," of "illuminating," of being "king." Snowball is savage and does eat his victims, just as any hero, symbolically speaking, must be aggressive and hostile until he commits and then assimilates his act. Snowball is self-sufficient and independent.

Maurice,[5] a common French name, is by its banality and lack of individuality representative of the character in the play: a creature lacking identity. Furthermore, *Mauros* is the Greek word for "black," and "Maurice" means "Moorish" or "dark-colored," indicating a "shadow," that is, Maurice's totally negative aspects. Other onomastic devices associated euphemistically with the *mort* sound in Maurice's name, suggest "death" or "dying."

Maurice is the youngest of the cellmates; like a child, he requires constant approval from his hero-father, Green Eyes. His hero represents his ideal, yet he does not dare identify with him openly, the difference between them being too great. Instead, he tries to emulate him. His attachment to Green Eyes is so great that such a relationship can only lead to stunted growth on the part of the adolescent, who will be kept in a permanent state of subjugation. Maurice is incapable of living his own life and finding his own personality. He can only live through Green Eyes. This kind of individual will offer his hero magnificent gestures. And, indeed, Maurice offers to murder Green Eyes's woman for him, but these outward gestures of courage merely mask the strength his conscious mind really lacks. The life Maurice ought to have lived runs away in the form of fantasies attributed to his hero figure or acted out by him. The collapse of Maurice's ideal, after Green Eyes has recounted his crime, leads to his destruction. He has merely lived in Green Eyes's shadow or, to state it another way, in a regressive state, and as such, has never really lived at all.

Maurice's regressive state, or his withdrawal from life, has disrupted the instinctual foundations of his personality, which has in turn led to a violent suppression of any incompatible tendencies within himself. There can, therefore, never be a struggle within him; no great and audacious act can take place; and, consequently, there can be no development or maturation. Furthermore, Maurice is the only character to walk barefoot. He is what is commonly referred to as a "tender foot," a boy who has not yet developed a personal standpoint.

One might say that Maurice suffers from an "Isaac complex." It must be recalled that Abraham was willing to sacrifice his only son Isaac to God. Maurice follows his father-hero Green Eyes as Isaac followed Abraham. Neither rebels; neither stands on his own two feet. Their impotence, their reliance on "father authority" or "conscience," "drowns the inner voice" or unconscious. "A reactionary identification with the father prevents the adolescent's struggle for independence" or, stated in other terms, the heroic deed so necessary for evolution and maturation.[6] Isaac was saved by divine intervention. Green Eyes watches Maurice's murder take place. He sees in Maurice's death the sacrifice of the sterile, unproductive, and parasitic aspects of himself. They symbolically wither and die, that the remaining aspects of himself may grow unhampered.

It is Maurice who accuses Lefranc of bringing disorder to the cell, of wanting to be like Green Eyes, of praising Snowball, and of denigrating Green Eyes in the same breath. When Lefranc accuses Maurice of bringing disorder to the cell, he denies this affirmation vehemently: "I can still vanish in the fog. I'm the kid who slips through walls."

Maurice is able to "disappear" and "slip through walls" because he is unformed, like an amoeba or jellyfish that can pass very easily from one form to another. Maurice owes his life to his hero, he says. This is true because without Green Eyes, who is the host, his parasitic existence would have long since caused his death. He censures Lefranc for "swallowing" the adventures of others, but this is as true for Maurice as it is for Lefranc—each sees it in the other, neither in himself. Lefranc is different; he is an intellectual, a poet. He will always be alone—the outcast. Maurice reacts to Lefranc's attitude because his very existence would be threatened were his hero to be "crippled." Each time Lefranc denigrates his hero, and by implication himself, Maurice is on defensive, and this attitude is manifested physically—Maurice pushes away an imaginary lock of hair from his forehead. Maurice unconsciously wishes to possess that lock of hair, since hair is taken to be a sign of a hero's virility, and the lack of it, a sign of emasculation. This means that Maurice is letting himself be cut off, devoured symbolically, by Green Eyes—his identity is being absorbed by another. He brushes his hair aside in a vain attempt to brush away his illusion.

Maurice offers to kill Green Eyes's woman in a supreme effort to prove his devotion to his hero-god. Maurice feels that she is his hero's enemy and, like a dragon, saps his vitality. In reality, she is sapping Maurice's vitality since she draws Green Eyes away from him. Maurice is living out his fantasies when he boasts of his future crime. After he kills Green Eyes's woman he will be a hero, an idol, and blood will flow: "I'll only have to transform myself into a rose to be picked." Maurice is so far removed from reality that he suffers the fate of many pseudoheroes—inflation. The rose in Genet's symbology refers to the criminal, the Harcamone type, for example, in *Miracle of the Rose.* Maurice could not possibly be transformed into the flower, which symbolizes the self and wholeness, since he lacks the audacity and courage to bring the struggle necessary to become a living being. The rose frequently represents the "unfolding soul" and indicates Maurice's desire for "completeness." Such unity, however, cannot be achieved without an active struggle on the part of the individual. Similarly, the hero in the thirteenth-century allegorical poem *Le Roman de la Rose* could not have reached the rose of his desire without a struggle between life's aiding and hindering forces. No such struggle takes place with Maurice, and so he will never be that rose.

When Green Eyes accepts the gift of the two cigarettes from Snowball, symbolizing his subservience to his god, Maurice's hero crumbles in his eyes. In a last moment of forgetfulness, and just as Lefranc pounces upon him, Maurice unconsciously runs to Green Eyes for protection. But Green Eyes is really no longer his hero and no longer casts a reflection upon him. All life-giving energy, therefore, has been withdrawn from Maurice. Maurice must die, and the symbolic death of the parasite is acted out on stage by Lefranc.

Lefranc, as his name indicates, should be the "frank one," but he is, until the end of the play, all but frank. His relationship to Green Eyes is also that of hero and hero worshiper. His identification with his hero goes even deeper, however. He not only wants to identify himself with Green Eyes, but he wants to become Green Eyes, thereby losing whatever identity he possesses. Maurice is formless; Lefranc has been formed but is unable to face his formation, which has become distorted as a result of his inability to come to grips with himself. Each time Lefranc puts on Green Eyes's jacket he blots out his own self. He not only symbolically stifles his inner voice by his act, but prevents any contact with outside forces, thereby becoming even more enmeshed in his illusion.

Lefranc is accused by Maurice of praying and saying Mass to pictures of great criminals hidden under his mattress. It is the ritualistic devotion of man to his god, of Lefranc to his heroes, and the hope of being transformed into one of them, that Genet here illustrates. A similar situation exists in Stendhal's *The Red and the Black* when Julien Sorel hides the picture of his hero Napoleon under his mattress. Julien Sorel is another unauthentic individual who wants to become someone else instead of being himself. Lefranc, the intellectual and the poet, is different from his fellow prisoners and because of this is rejected by them.

Every word that Lefranc utters in the beginning of the play is the opposite of what he really believes. His praise of Snowball is an attempt to make Green Eyes feel inferior and, by the same token, himself feel superior. These are traps Lefranc is setting for Green Eyes. Lefranc calls Snowball exotic; he says Snowball shines, radiates, that he is a master criminal. Green Eyes has only one crime to his name and even this is unauthentic. Such are the underhanded methods Lefranc uses to undermine his hero's confidence, to cut him up, so to speak. Lefranc's main desire is to isolate his hero, to prevent any contact with outside forces: either with Snowball or Green Eyes's woman. In this way he can take over his identity and so become his "brother."

Strangely enough, Lefranc sums himself up perfectly when he boasts

"I can become a cyclone and tear you apart" (*MD,* 162). The violent winds and rains of a cyclone center around a calm center. Wind which can be a productive and life-giving force can also be a terrible destroyer, as can foundationless instincts. Lefranc's psychic center has no roots and travels around in circles. It longs for just those foundations that it lacks. During its journey, the psychic cyclone becomes more and more violent. In the end the destruction it wreaks is pointless, as Lefranc's destruction of Maurice is pointless, since he does not achieve his desired goal, which is "friendship" and "union" with Green Eyes, his hero.

Furthermore, a cyclone is a tropical typhoon. The Greek monster Typhon, the god of the wind, is Set, the evil one in Egyptian mythology. It was Set, Osiris' brother, who lured him and then locked Osiris in a chest, dismembered his body, and scattered the pieces. Isis, with the help of Anubis, collected the pieces but was unable to find the phallus and Osiris, having lost his regenerative powers, remained a "phantom" and was relegated to the underworld where he weighed the souls of the dead. His son Horus, symbolizing the new generation, the new law, battled with Set. Such a replacement of authority had to take place for evolution to occur. So Set, though "evil," served in the end for forces of "good."[7]

Lefranc in many respects can be considered the Set of our story. He looks with envy at Green Eyes (Osiris); he loves him at the same time. In fact, Lefranc admits his "evil" intentions at the end of the play. In writing the letters to Green Eyes's woman, Lefranc declares, "I was taking your place. . . . I got into your skin. . . ." Lefranc wants to remain in the cell with Green Eyes. He wants to separate the cell from the world, to isolate it "from the entire prison," to prevent even "a single breath of air to come in from the outside." Lefranc murders Maurice to prove his heroism, to win Green Eyes's admiration and friendship. His action is not heroic, nor is it a "complete crime," because he is unable to face the reason for his act. But when Lefranc says, "I wanted to become what you were. . . . My misfortune comes from something deeper. It comes from myself. . . . I am really alone . . ." (*MD,* 146, 161), he becomes heroic, since strength and audacity (the act) were required to see clearly into himself.

Lefranc emerges as the hero of our story. He is the "actor," the "rebel" who wants to destroy Snowball's power. He is, however, doomed to exile and solitude. But he has also lived fully because he is able to face the consequences of his action. Lefranc most of all reflects Genet's own spirit. He is like Lucifer—the "light-bringer."

Green Eyes's name is also indicative of his personality. His eyes are like "windows" in the Platonic sense—they look out on life; they are the soul's eyes. They are green because, like cat's eyes, they see in the dark. Green Eyes is both a hero and a hero worshiper. His god is Snowball, a sun-god who traverses the skies or the upper regions of the prison or fortress.

Green Eyes's attitude is ambivalent in the beginning. His desire to give his woman away or to ask for her death is a symbolic wish to be divested of certain aspects of himself. It is also the wish to destroy the female principle or the mother aspect in general. On the other hand, Green Eyes resents Lefranc's attempt to win his woman away from them. The desire to keep the principle is still there.

Before his crime, Green Eyes always had flowers in his teeth, he says. He was strong. Teeth represent aggressiveness and are a necessary corollary to creativity, to physical and psychic nourishment. This is why Snowball ate his victims—he assimilated them and was nourished by them symbolically. But Green Eyes, rather than benefiting from his crime, was emasculated by it. He said he lost his "lilac" in the process, his germinating and productive aspect—his phallus. He complains that he is no longer the "man" he had been. Now he is too "pale," too "white"; he is like the moon revolving around the earth and living through the rays cast by his sun, Snowball.

When Green Eyes narrates his unauthentic crime, which his conscious mind can never accept, and further reveals that he has tried to be another: a cat, a horse, a panther, a savage like his hero Snowball—he realizes the dangers involved in not facing his present situation and in not being able to see his action through to the very end. He cannot assimilate his crime. He tries to forget about it; to relive the days before he committed the crime. He cannot, he realizes, go back. His anguish is so great that he begins to dance in spirals on stage. And as he dances he wears a look of extreme pain and suffering. Green Eyes dances for the same reason that Maurice walks barefoot. He tries like the dancing dervishes, through the swirling motions of his feet, to come into contact with mother earth and, by analogy, with his most primitive being. It is only this primitive being that speaks the truth.

The strength he needs to face his acts has been mustered. Green Eyes is now able to see through himself and so unite the conflicting aspects of himself, bringing about the necessary "calm" he seeks. He says he is broken, that he is in pieces, but that he will "put himself back together . . . ," that he will not "remain in pieces . . . ," that he will "rebuild himself" and "fix himself up like new." And Green Eyes is put back together again with the admission of his subservience to Snowball, that is, by accepting the two cigarettes, he becomes authentic. He says: "It was only when I saw that everything was irremediable that I quieted down. I've only just accepted it. I had to be total" (*MD,* 162). But like Osiris, Green Eyes will be reborn imperfectly, his "lilac" having been stolen. He can never be on a par with Snowball because he lacks the solar energy, and, as Osiris, will remain as judge and weigher of souls in the underworld. And Green Eyes assumes just such a pose when he stands on a stoollike basin and watches Lefranc murder Maurice. He judges Lefranc as Osiris judged those shadows that passed before him. Green Eyes has come to grips with himself with the aid of Lefranc, the force of evil; he sees himself for what he is and accepts his limitations. He will bear the weight of the cell, but Snowball will bear "the same weight for the entire fortress . . ." (*MD,* 154).

The biblical story of Adam and his sons, Cain and Abel, is also reenacted in *Deathwatch.* Green Eyes is Adam, who is docile in his worship of God. Green Eyes's crime never amounted to anything since it was not thought out or reasoned but merely instinctual. He did not set out to destroy or to change. His crime did not require courage or audacity. Adam's crime of eating the apple was also unauthentic since it was Eve who pushed him to it.[8] Snowball then would be God, the creator of the entire picture, the mastermind, the power, the one who brings about Maurice's fall, Green Eyes's subservience, and Lefranc's exile; in like manner, God brought about Adam's fall, Abel's murder, and Cain's exile. Lefranc becomes Cain, the rebel, the outcast; Maurice is Abel, the docile one who adored both his father and God. It was Cain, the "tiller of the ground," whose offering to God was not accepted; Abel, the "keeper of the sheep," whose offspring was accepted by God. Abel's gift, however, was nonproductive; he was merely a "keeper" of traditions, of the status quo, of society, of relationships; he was not a producer, just as Maurice is not a producer but merely a "shadow" and "follower." Cain's offering came from the earth, the "fruit of the ground," and he had to dig deep and work the soil with the sweat of his brow. Lefranc has to burrow deep within himself to find humanity, to perform his "audacious" act that will result in the acceptance of his solitude. Cain killed Abel out of vengeance and a spirit of rebellion aimed not only against Adam his father, but against God, that is, authority. Cain was jealous of God's attention to Adam and to Abel; Lefranc, of Snowball's favoring Green Eyes and Maurice. Cain

(Lefranc) wanted to win the affection of God (Snowball) and Adam (Green Eyes) and so destroyed Abel (Maurice), the one he thought prevented such a relationship. Lefranc destroys Maurice in order to become Green Eyes's "friend." Cain was exiled for his act as Lefranc is thrust out of the cell for his. Cain became a "fugitive vagabond"; he took his punishment and paid for his crime by bearing his solitude. Cain was not destroyed by God."[9] Lefranc's type will not be destroyed either.

What Genet is telling his audiences in *Deathwatch,* one of his most stirring plays, is that the unproductive elements within the individual as within society must be expunged. Life must be faced with "courage" and "audacity," and, above all, "creatively." Such men as Lefranc, the pariah, are necessary. It is they who force society to take stock of itself. God did not destroy the criminal, Cain, because he knew that without the rebellious, evolution and change would never occur.

Chapter Eight
The Maids

From a certain point onward there is no longer any turning back. That is the point that must be reached.

—Franz Kafka, *The Great Wall of China*

Les Bonnes (*The Maids*) was first produced by Louis Jouvet in 1947 at the Athénée Theatre.[1] Like *Deathwatch,* Genet's second theatrical endeavor was a classically constructed tragedy. Unlike classical drama, however, which deals with whole people who grow as the play progresses, *The Maids* presents three formless phantoms or shadows who are systematically peeled of their coverings.

In *Deathwatch* Genet introduced his audiences to three criminals on stage, and one master criminal, Snowball, who was never seen. In *The Maids,* a similar situation is dramatized. On stage, there are two maids and a Madame; and there is also Madame's lover, Monsieur, whom the audience never sees and around whom Madame's life centers. Madame and her two maids are faceless: they have no identities. They are like many-faceted diamonds with one facet shining in the light while the other side remains in virtual shadow. One side, then, exists as a reflection of the other, just as one character lives in *The Maids* by virtue of the others. Each character is what the other makes her out to be and what she thinks herself to be. Each interweaves her complex pattern of behavior with the other, confusing, interfering, and virtually destroying any "realistic" interactions or interrelationships. Not one character in *The Maids* exists by herself as an entity.

The event that inspired Genet's *The Maids* occurred in 1933 in Le Mans. Two sisters, Lea and Christine Papin, working for an upper-class family, brutally murdered their employers, Madame Lancelin and her daughter, without any known cause. During the trial it was revealed that the two sisters, who lived like virtual recluses, had been inhumanly treated by their mistresses. Because the gory evidence brought out during the trial favored the establishment, such notable political and literary figures as Simone de Beauvoir conveyed their distress at what they believed to be the exploitation of the proletariat. Jacques Lacan's exploration of the Papin sisters' psychological condition and which he identified with paranoia, suggested that one of the prime reasons for the murder of their employers was their unconscious homosexual leanings. To repress these powers creates an emotionally volatile situation, their murderous instincts were frequently directed against a surrogate figure who may be associated with the beloved. By killing their employers, Lacan maintained, they were destroying the two women upon whom they projected and so, in effect, were really killing themselves.[2]

Genet's intent, however, transcended political and sociological expediency. He was not interested in fighting for the rights of domestic servants, he wrote in "How to Play *The Maids*," particularly since they have their own unions. Rather than limit theater by locking it into political or sociological ideologies, Genet sought to expand its dimension, encouraging it to inhabit both conscious and unconscious domains, timeless and spaceless spheres. Like Artaud, Genet felt distaste for Western theatrical conventions and was drawn to Japanese, Chinese, and Balinese symbolic stage events. Actors must not identify with their characters, he felt, particularly since Genet sought to abolish the very notion of characters, along with the psychological conventions associated with them. A performer may then "become a sign charged with signs" and became "as remote as possible from what they are meant first to signify." Genet wanted to create a work "in which nothing is said but everything portended."[3]

Illusion and Reality

Too involved to be recounted briefly, the play revolves around two maids, Solange and Claire, sisters who play the game of impersonating their Madame and her relationship with her lover, Monsieur. Out of hatred, the maids plot to kill her, fail, and one sister kills the other sister, the impersonator.

Madame, Solange, and Claire all are alienated from the real world; they have not been able to function in it and so have resorted to living a game in a dreamworld. Dressed in gaudy attire, Madame lives out her fantasy with Monsieur. She paints a glowing picture of her martyrdom, her saintliness and herosim, and plans to devote her life to him. Madame is kind to her maids and gives them her old clothes. She loves them as objects, just as Mme Lysiane (*Quarrel of Brest*) loved people.

Solange and Claire lead fantasy lives not only as each other but as Madame. They despise their serfdom, their Madame, their sordid life, and they dream of being famous criminals—the hero type once again. They visualize themselves on a balcony, which implies the edge of an abyss, being cheered by the multitude. Clearly, their fantasies have been carried to the extreme limit.

As there is no absolute identity, so there is no more absolute reality than there is absolute good or evil. Reality is appearance and changes with each person's view of it. In the theater, which is "illusion" par excellence, audiences may be held in bondage and suspense by theatrical reality. Genet warns the spectators every now and then not to be duped by the "trap" set by both actor and author: not to believe the supreme form of make-believe, that is, the big lie. Yet, both author and actor want audiences to believe. Such is the paradox.

Genet is intrigued by the artifice and the sham of the theater as he had been by the betrayal and deceit of crime. He wants the lie in the theater to be carried as far as possible and so originally declared that *The Maids* should be played by men. Louis Jouvet, however, refused to comply, and Genet acquiesced. Had the characters been played by men, the confusion between illusion and reality would have been that much greater. Men would have been playing at being women, who would in turn have been playing at being maids, who would themselves have been playing at being each other, who then would have been playing at being Madame, who would have been playing at being part of Madame's dreamworld.

Sartre pointed out that there are continual ramifications to each character in *The Maids,* that there is a constant interchange of truths and lies that he calls "circular sophistry." This type of reasoning, inherited from the ancient Skeptics, which Sartre calls "whirligigs," maintains that truth leads to the lie and vice versa. He further states that "The mind that enters one of these vicious circles goes round and round, unable to stop." Sartre quotes from Epimenides to illustrate this point." "Epimenides says that Cretans are liars. But he is a Cretan. Therefore he lies. Therefore Cretans are not liars. Therefore, he speaks the truth. Therefore, Cretans are liars. Therefore, he lies. . . ."[4]

Everything in *The Maids* points to this kind of circulatory or ambulatory thinking. All is dual. Even the title is double. The word "maids," in French *bonnes,* means both "maids" and "the good ones." Solange and Claire are maids of a sort, but not "the good ones," since they reveal only their hideously deformed aspects. The names of the protagonists are also dual. Claire means light, luminous, yet she casts her shadow all about. Solange, as was pointed out in the discussion of *Our Lady of the Flowers,* consists of *sol* meaning "sun" and "earth," and *ange,* meaning "angel"—another example of the spiritual and physical split within the character. The fact that Madame has no personal names makes her an impersonal being, while at the same time she is a personal being for the maids. She is a symbol, a function, as is her lover, Monsieur.

Solange and Claire, who are sisters, both hate and love each other. They also hate and love their Madame, who is beautiful and rich. Without realizing what they are doing, each one projects herself onto the women. By so doing, they obliterate in the others what they hate in themselves, and magnify in the others what they love in themselves, divesting themselves still further of any identity they might have had. In addition, each maid will play the other maid and the Madame because each exists as a reflection of the other—never as an individual per se.

Claire will not play herself, but Solange and Madame. And Solange in turn will play at being herself, Madame, and Claire. Madame will play herself. She will also play herself as she imagines herself to be in her fantasy world. There are, then, not three characters in this play, Claire, Solange, and Madame, but eight, each one of whom is trying to find her identity in the next person and yet never quite able to do so.

Technically speaking, the rotation of the roles, the loss of identities, becomes more and more precipitous with the rising intensity of the emotions, which range from love to brutalizing sadomasochism. The play swirls toward an orgy of sexual excitement; then the pace slackens only to reach another peak—the climax—the murder.

Genet's symbols propel his drama along. His creation of contrasts lends visual excitement to the tale, heightening pace and suspense. The sensuousness of his prose, the constant reference to the senses of smell and touch, the visual images, serve to attract the spectator as the carnivorous flower attracts its victim. Once the spectator is enmeshed in the drama, he becomes identified with the shadows peopling the stage—and there he is held until deliberately repelled by Genet, only to be clutched again a moment later. The spectator becomes part of a ritualistic and religious ceremony of death—and death is the extreme travesty.

The Travesty—A Game

Though *The Maids* is a one-act play, it can be divided into five parts: 1) the play-acting or game carried on by the two maids, Solange and Claire, which ends with the ringing of the alarm clock; (2) the continuation of the game until the ringing of the telephone; 3) Madame's entrance; 4) Madame's exit; 5) the finale.[5]

The play is set in Madame's rococo bedroom with its Louis XV furniture, its laces, its bed, a window covered with heavy drapes, and a profusion of flowers. The sets, as designed by Christian Berard for the 1948 production, gave a stifling and claustrophobic effect.

Claire and Solange are supposed to be cleaning up Madame's bedroom in her absence. Instead, they are at their favorite game—playing at being Madame. The audience, however, does not know that Solange and Claire are both maids, but thinks that one of them is the maid and the other, Madame. The audience will become aware of their identities as the scene progresses.

Claire, in her slip, is talking in Madame's voice and orders her sister Solange, who is playing Claire, to bring back "these eternal gloves" (MD, 76); they are rubber gloves that belong in the kitchen. The gloves are not only a symbol of servitude, but a cover behind which the maids' true intent can be hidden—one of the many masks used during the course of the play. The maids continually identify themselves with their masks, whatever it may be at the moment, and to such an extent that they break the ties with themselves still further.

Solange-Claire obeys Claire-Madame. She is called by Claire-Madame, however, who orders her to bring her white dress, jewels, and patent leather shoes. Solange-Clair spits on the shoes to bring out their shine, but the fact that she spits on them is a manifestation of her disgust-hate toward both Madame and her sister, Claire-Madame is revolted by this "veil of saliva" which will envelop her foot—another mask to cover her identity. Solange-Claire kneels to put on Claire-Madame's shoe and enjoys the subservience of this act.

Claire-Madame accuses Solange-Claire of carrying on an illicit affair with Mario, the milkman. Solange-Claire accuses Claire-Madame of having written letters accusing Monsieur, Madame's lover, of false theft. As a result, he is in jail. Now, Claire-Madame states, in a supreme act of dedication, that she will follow her lover to the end of the world.

Clothing is again used to cover up real identities, thereby adding more confusion to the situation. Claire-Madame wants to put on her white dress because "the white dress is the mourning of queens." Solange-Claire, however, wants her to wear the red one, because it would serve her "widowhood even better." White is the immaculate color of the Virgin and red, the color of communion wine. The religious ritual begins.

Claire-Madame will wear the red dress but is revolted when Solange-Claire touches her to help her on with it. Unconsciously, she has donned the "immaculate white dress," in reality, the red one, underlining the dualism. Claire-Madame continues, "You smell the wild beast, the filth of your job, your room with its two iron beds, its night table, its little altar with its plaster statue of the Holy Virgin." The more she talks, the more Solange-Claire is attracted by her beauty, her body, her holiness. She touches her again. "I am a more beautiful Virgin, Claire. . . ." says Claire-Madame, who strikes Solange-Claire, declaring, "Your contact is impure." She cannot bear the contact of dirt on purity, evil on good. She is poles apart from herself; her spiritual half is so inflated that it has lost all contact with her physical self.

This contact or lack of it, these distances and interchanges, not only symbolize human beings without identity, but also the distances that separate men from men, and men from God—the distance between the Virgin and the plaster effigy, which is as false as are Madame, Solange, and Claire; between employer and employee; between the accepted and the outcast; between the criminal and the saint.

The game must go on. Solange and Claire must kill Madame. A bitter sexual battle of invectives and hatreds, of grimaces and disgust, ensues. The game is going well and Solange-Claire reaches a paroxysm of hate: "I hate you! . . . Your chest . . . of all ivory! Your things . . . of gold! Your feet . . . of amber!" She spits on the red dress with almost orgiastic delight and erotic rapture. White, gold, and ivory—the spiritual colors of purity and royalty, goodliness and saintliness—are used to describe the sensual thighs and chest. Solange slaps her sister and says: "Claire is there, clearer than ever. Luminous!" She belittles Claire-Madame's affair with a common thief, an affair Madame paints in glamorous colors.

The alarm clock rings. Reality blusters its way into the sordid game the two sisters are playing. Madame will return shortly. They are annoyed with each other for not having been able to murder Madame. The travesty Solange says: "You can resemble yourself, now. Take back your face. Go on, Claire, be my sister again" (*MD,* 76).

Claire puts on her little black dress, arranges the key in the secretary, the flowers, and slowly wanders into the game again. "Let me talk. Let me empty myself," declares Solange. She describes the balcony on which Claire nightly parades as she salutes like a queen the "multitudes" before her, wrapped in drapes or in a bedspread of lace; then she contemplates herself in the mirror, seeing her myriad reflections. There is a fundamental need on the part of the maids to attract, to win attention, to be accepted. They will become great murderesses; they will be saluted.

But the maids are *really* in danger now. Claire has written anonymous letters denouncing Monsieur. To prime herself with information to write these letters, she stole some of Monsieur's letters to Madame. But Solange accuses Claire of having stolen these letters to live her "secret adventure," because everyone dreams of a secret adventure with a convict. Solange was too cowardly to write these letters. Yet she kept Monsieur's letters to Madame instead of returning them after the anonymous letters were written, because she was in love with Monsieur; and she, too, liked to play Madame, sacrificing herself for her lover. The more dangerous the game becomes, the greater is the sisters' excitement and the more intense is their sadomasochistic orgy.

Claire becomes frightened as violence is heaped upon violence. "It is I you are aiming at through Madame, I am the one who is in danger." She admits that she wants to free her sister because Claire is absolutely possessed by Madame. She loves her sister and yet knows that Claire would be the first to denounce her if she killed Madame.

The telephone rings, and reality again intrudes in this heinous game. Monsieur has been freed and asks the maids to tell Madame to meet him at Bilboquet's. The maids now fear discovery since "Everything is going to talk." Madame will know they wrote the letters because of the "curtains marked by your shoulders, the mirrors by my face, the light accustomed to our faces . . ." (*MD*, 93).

They must kill Madame. Claire has had enough of being "the spider, the umbrella case, and the sordid nun without a god, without a family." Solange, too, has had enough of "our resemblance. . . ." Solange, however, sees herself not only as a frightened and hunted animal, but with disgust and anger at her physical and spiritual servitude. She is what Madame has made of her and vice versa. Madame is what the maids have made of her. In the mirrors, Claire sees her face thrown back at her like a "bad odor."

Claire will kill Madame; she will be crowned and become a heroine in crime. Together, "we will be the eternal couple, the criminal and the saint. We will be saved, Solange, I swear to you. . . ." Then in a love-duet Solange asks Claire to rest; she will carry her up to her crib. The tenderness of their words, as contrasted with the preceding violence, makes the sexual overtones all the more pronounced. Claire tries to sleep but gets up to prepare the ten pellets of gardenol to poison Madame's tea. She says, "We will sing! We will bury her. . . ." They will cut her up into little pieces as Osiris was cut up. "One must eat. To be strong" (*MD,* 99). The communion will be accomplished; the wine and host will be swallowed; the ritualistic murder will take place, and Solange and Claire will be free to be reborn as one. A nervous laughter is heard, and Madame, covered with furs, enters.

Madame describes in glowing terms (her interpretation) Monsieur's arrest, the anonymous letters, his innocence. She will be a saint, martyr; she will carry the cross, give up furs, jewels, everything, to follow Monsieur. Claire brings the poisoned tea. Madame will not drink it, however, because she is going to be a saint and as such is living out her fantasy and renunciation. Each time the maids offer her the tea, she refuses with another excuse. As soon as Madame hears Monsieur has been freed, she orders a cab and her furs. No tea for Madame; she will drink champagne with Monsieur.

Madame exits. "Madame has escaped us, Claire!" Solange says. Solange and Claire are frightened at being discovered, at the thought of being simple little criminals rather than queens of the underworld. Should they run away? Where? Why? Since they have not murdered Madame in reality and are incapable of functioning as real human beings in a real society, Solange will have to kill Claire-Madame to bring about her release. The more monstrous and brutalizing is their conversation about the murder, the more pleasure and excitement both experience. "I am quivering, I am shivering with pleasure, Claire, I'm going to neigh with joy!" In a lyrical tirade, Solange runs the gamut of emotions: love, hate, tenderness, viciousness. The ceremony begins, and the hangman will "rock" her, the spectators will acclaim her. She is lost in a haze, a maze. "Now we are Mademoiselle Solange Lemercier. . . . The famous criminal." Claire-Madame declares that, after her death, "Solange, you will keep me in you. . . . You will assume our two existences alone" (*MD,* 139). This time the game will reach its culmination, Claire-Madame must sleep. She lies down on Madame's bed and drinks the tea. Solange faces the audience, immobile, "her hands joined as though by handcuffs."

The Black Mass

The game played by the two maids is a ritual, a religious ceremony, a Black Mass, as Sartre wrote, a display of magic. In the religious ceremony "introjection" of God takes place during communion; the wine becomes blood and flows through the veins of the partaker; the host is flesh and is eaten by the believer so that God can be reborn and live within them. Symbolically, then, there is an interchange of the most holy kind.

Genet's characters number three, a trinity, thereby carrying the religious symbolism still further. Each being absorbs another and is absorbed by the other; each feeds upon another and is fed by him. Though feeding on someone else implies the destruction of that other person, the one being nourished grows stronger. The stronger of the two, however, will break this tenuous equation and will kill the other, absorbing from the other while doing so. The one who dies will still live in the one who has absorbed him and will be reborn within him. Such a cycle has gone on as long as man has lived on earth.[6] The murder takes place on stage as part of their ritualistic game, which is repeated over and over again: Solange-Claire will absorb Claire-Madame and by doing so will be released of all she projects onto the other.

The faceless beings Genet has created will not act and react as in an adult world, but will unconsciously withdraw in time and space to a childhood realm where they feel they can find safety and protection. They will play a game, which implies fun and frolic, but which turns out to be a monstrously solid ritual. In this rich merry-go-round, Genet wields his marionettes as he parades them out of conscious reality and introduces them to their unconscious. Deeper and deeper he thrusts them into their Dantesque inferno, cutting surfaces, skinning layers, revealing ever another aspect as their inner journey progresses.

In *The Maids* Genet created beings identified with their illusions, but who were able to a certain extent to function in the workaday world. In *The Balcony,* one of the most exciting plays written in our century, Genet goes a step further, featuring beings who reject the world in which they live and who choose to make their home in a "house of illusion."

Chapter Nine
The Balcony

> The dream is a second life. I was never able to pierce those doors of ivory or of horn which separate us from the invisible world without shuddering. The first instance of sleep is the image of death: a nebulous numbness seizes our mind, and we cannot determine the precise instant when the *I,* under another form, continues the work of life. A vague underground region lights up little by little: and from here, the pale and gravely immobile figures which inhabit the region of limbo, liberate themselves from the shadow and the night. Then the picture takes shape, a new clarity illuminates it and puts these bizarre apparitions into play—the world of the Spirits has opened for us.
>
> —Gérard de Nerval, *Aurélia*

The premiere of *Le Balcon* (*The Balcony*) took place on 22 April 1957 in London at the Arts Theatre Club.[1] Genet found much to criticize in Peter Zadek's direction of his play, as he did later in the New York, Paris, and Berlin productions. In Genet's introduction to the 1962 edition of *The Balcony,* entitled "How to Play *The Balcony,*" he wrote that the scenes in his play must succeed each other as though each one fitted into the next. Furthermore, every actor must perform in an exaggerated manner, yet some passages must be played more naturally than others to underline the contrasts. Genet wanted to keep his audiences in a state of suspense. They must, therefore, never know whether the occurrences on stage and the feelings of the protagonists are feigned or real.[2]

The Balcony is one giant metaphor with infinite prismatic reflections and reverberations. Critics have throughout the years pointed up its comic, tragic, satiric, ironic, and parodic elements, and emphasizing as well its political, religious, sociological, semiotic, deconstructionist, and hermeneutic sides. These views may all be considered valid since *The Balcony* is, as Genet wrote, a "glorification of the Image and the Reflection," encouraging audiences and readers to project whatever they wish upon the work of art, which it is. The last laugh, however, is

Genet's, as is the supreme joy of entrapping those who frame *The Balcony* within their own circumscribed certitudes, their restrictive constrictions, keys, and codes. Creation, whatever its nature, is for Genet fluid and flowing, continuously shaping and reshaping itself in a protean manner.

As one great metaphor, *The Balcony* is reminiscent in some respects of Paul Claudel's theatrical metaphor, *Partage de midi* (Break of noon). Genet possessed the same vitality, energy, power to stimulate, and searing fire that Claudel had, the same painful split within the soul that, like a ritual march, leads through destruction to salvation. Genet's and Claudel's stylistic techniques are also comparable: both men create a rhythmic rapport between spectators and actors through assonance, alliteration, repetition of words and phrases, and antithesis, not only as far as the meanings of words are concerned, but also in their effects upon the senses. Such hypnotic use of rhythms and sounds with their balances and stresses creates a visceral empathy among writers, actors, audiences, and readers alike.

Comparisons between Pirandello's theater within the theater must not be omitted. For example, the characters in *Six Characters in Search of an Author* are really seeking spectators. Although Pirandello may conceive of a father when he wrote the play, it takes another/spectator to give this being reality. The actor incarnating the director views the performer portraying the Father as the Father, and the Father playing his role does likewise. A similar situation occurs in *Tonight We Improvise:* the audience attempts to distinguish the actors portraying their stage roles from those performing in the play within the play. So, too, are Genet's complex beings in *The Balcony* conceived, but with an added twist. His intent is to deceive the naive spectators, thereby divesting them of mimesis while adding to the factitious nature of the dramatic spectacle by mingling the literal and the imagined activities of his stage personalities. In this manner he succeeds in intensifying the ambiguity of the stage play as well as the malaise of the spectators/voyeurs.

The Balcony as a symbol has appeared before in *Our Lady of the Flowers, The Maids, Funeral Rites,* and *Quarrel of Brest.* The symbol acts as a dividing line, a *partage* between two types of existence, always in conflict for Genet and always dangerous: spirit and matter, illusion and reality, life and death, the outer and the inner world. If one steps too far forward on a balcony one is likely to fall off and be dashed into an abyss or sink beneath the ground unto death. On the other hand, since the balcony stands above the crowd, above ground, it dominates everything around. If one remains within its boundaries and above life, so to speak, one is alienated and removed from life's sources. A balance, therefore, must be maintained for the average person between illusion or spirituality (on the balcony) and reality and the material (on the ground).

In Genet's narratives, his protagonists worship the criminal heroes who have become divinities for them. These supermen who communed with stars and planets and penetrated the mysteries of the earth, and for whom no mineral or botanical language is unknown, make life worth while for the lonely and downtrodden characters. Harcamone, Erik, Quarrel give the wretched of the earth a *raison d'être,* a hope for better things to come through them. The novels in many respects represent the product of Genet's youthful attitude, his fire and energy, his desire to change the world by destroying it. Genet's theater, beginning with *Deathwatch,* reveals the mature and meditative side of the author. A master literary craftsman, as much at home in the theater as in the novel, Genet cuts the lyrical tirades present in his early works to a minimum in the plays; the most important themes are dealt with objectively; passions are controlled. Genet now looks bravely onto the world, as savage and sordid, as lonely and disheartening as it may be. His illusionless realm has been accepted as Cain accepted his lot.

In the *Miracle of the Rose* and in *Quarrel of Brest,* Genet told of his mystic experiences. In *The Balcony,* he transforms his religious experience into a codified theatrical technique with its own ritual and ceremony. In *The Balcony* distances are maintained, as they are in *The Maids* and *Deathwatch,* in order to conjure up a feeling of awesomeness and religiosity. Furthermore, Genet wrote that *The Balcony* should be played "with the solemnity of a Mass in a most beautiful cathedral. . . ."

A play for Genet was supposed to provoke a religious experience. In ancient times during performances of plays by Aeschylus, Euripides, and Sophocles, spectators frequently sensed a certain affinity with the divine, a mysterious presence living within them. The original religious experiences these ancient peoples felt in theaters or elsewhere became, throughout the centuries, codified. The institution of the Christian church, for example, evolved a series of symbols which, when ritualized and turned into a ceremony (invocations, incantations, sacrifice, meditation, rosary-saying, communion, pilgrimages, and prayer) repeated daily or weekly, became a form of, or activated, a religious experience.

Likewise, in *The Balcony,* the rituals enacted on stage are to act as potent forces in provoking a religious experience. At the same time, Genet dramatizes and satirizes the functions of certain institutions that wield and have wielded enormous power over peoples over the years: the church, the magistrature, the army, the police, the bordello. The figures representative of these functions (the bishop, the judge, the general, police chief, the madame) are already familiar characters in Genet's creative world. In *The Balcony,* however, they take a greater stature and broader significance.

The political motifs incised in *The Balcony*—the power struggle between opposing social and political institutions and groups—were inspired, Genet wrote, by incidents in Franco's Spain: "the revolutionary who castrated himself was the symbol of all Republicans who have acknowledged their defeat. From that point onward, however, my play went one way, while Spain went another."[3]

Other affinities between historical events and *The Balcony* will be briefly reviewed: the mausoleum constructed to honor the Chief of Police and his supporters may be associated with the memorial erected for the deed of the Spanish Civil War built at the Valle de los Caidos (The valley of the fallen) and dedicated by Franco in 1959. The military repression by the French of the Algerians during their uprising in 1954 may have been obliquely alluded to in *The Balcony.* Although the pros and cons of the anecdote (or anecdotes), political or otherwise, have been and will be argued ad infinitum, it is not reality that Genet seeks to represent on stage, despite the Brechtian interpretations some critics have sought to impose upon *The Balcony.* The event, Genet stated, is merely the starting point: "the ultimate sublimation of any commonplace event is through poetry. It is through poetry that any work of literature attains its highest realization. . . . Unless it [an event] is transformed, transmuted into poetry, it is nothing."[4]

That Genet instructs his directors to create decor and costumes that appear real, is his way of destroying mimesis, of emphasizing the giant hoax on illusion that is his play. What appears to be a brothel, in fact, is a theater. The ambiguity of the characters is also a factor with which one must contend in a society in which people go to the theater and may be influenced by what they see. Theater in this regard has a social role. What that is exactly is a mystery: "the process of the theater reflecting upon the theater turns into a concurrent chain of reflections on society."[5] According to Bernard Dort, *The Balcony* may be viewed as a theater or a representation: the theater being both subject matter and the mirror image through which the subject is refracted, thereby increasing interaction and metacommunication between the framed and unframed activities. A *mise-en-abyme, The Balcony* celebrates theater in order to destroy it.

Let us also add to the various views mentioned above the game element implicit in *The Balcony* and the excitement such intense activity generates. As Johan Huizinga remarked: "In play, there is something 'at play' which transcends the immediate needs of life."[6] As audiences view those in contest, victims and victors provoking each other in the *temenos*—that sacred space which is the stage—they are both caught up and confused by what they view in the closed- yet open-framed existences before them. The matriarchal/patriarchal society in Genet's house of illusion, however, is brought to life only to be destroyed so as to be reborn to the theater in a new and perhaps even more ambiguous mirror/reality.

The Plot

The Balcony, an extraordinarily imaginative play, includes nine tableaux and a cast of twenty. The curtains part on a sacristy formed by three blood-red screens placed one next to the other. An enormous Spanish crucifix painted in *trompe-l'oeil* is visible, along with a mirror that reflects an unmade bed, a stable, and an armchair on which black pants, a shirt, and a jacket have been placed. The Bishop is seated and speaks to Madame Irma and a penitent. When he rises in all of his grandeur and eminence with his miter, surplice, laces, and brocades, he looks enormous. He is wearing *cothurni*[7] and his shoulders are padded to give him more height, thereby dignity and authority.

The Bishop is irritated because the penitent has confessed only six sins, but he seems satisfied when she tells him that they were "deadly" sins. He begins a peroration on sin, desire, and evil, and in lofty terms declares, "I saw there the greedy longing for transgression. In flooding it, evil all at once baptized it. . . . But our holiness lies only in our being able to forgive you your sins."[8]

In a less theatrical tone the Bishop expresses his hope that the penitent's sins were not actually "real," for if they were, he will be in a "mess." Returning again to his sanctimonious tone, he assures all present that within these walls there is no possibility of evil.

Slowly, the penitent, with the help of another woman, Madame Irma, removes the Bishop's fineries: his surplice, miter, and laces. Just before they finish, the Bishop asks to be left alone. In front of the mirror now, he holds up and kisses his surplice, and thanks the laces and other accessories for having permitted him to fulfill his functions in solitude.

A volley of machine-gun fire now intrudes. A revolution is taking place outside. Mme Irma and the penitent remove the Bishop's *cothurni,* his padded shoulders—he has become man-sized. And as he looks at his costume on the ground, his religious vestments which had protected him from "reality," that is, from the outside world, the audience is suddenly shocked into awareness. The spectators realize that they are not present in the sacristy, but are rather in Mme Irma's brothel, her "house of illusions" called "The Grand Balcony." The Bishop is no bishop, but a gas man attired as a bishop, who can only enjoy sexual fulfillment when acting the role of a prince of the church. Mme Irma supplies all the accouterments, furnishings, accessories, actors, and actresses. Her clients, or "visitors" as she calls them, supply scenarios that they can change to suit themselves. However, both employees and "visitors" must adhere to strict regulations and etiquette. By thus stressing the literal function of her house of illusion, Mme Irma is accentuating the dimensionality of fantasy, thus heightening the sexual delight experienced by the "visitors" making their way into her closed institution.

The succeeding tableaux dramatize similar situations and asymmetrical relationships and layerings of experience. The audience sees a judge crawling on his belly toward a half-naked woman whose foot is extended in his direction. She draws back as he advances. "Not yet! Lick! First lick . . . ," she says. Later, a General loves his horse, who is played by a beautiful red-headed girl wearing a black corset, black stockings, and high heeled shoes. As she brings the General his complete uniform, consisting of sword, boots, two-cornered hat, jacket, pants, *cothurni,* and padded shoulders, she neighs, rears, and finally kneels before him like a circus horse. She tells him of the war he has fought, of his tenderness, his heroism.

The audience learns that in Mme Irma's other studios, which are visible via a televisionlike contraption, there are a succession of scenes: a leper who is being cured by the Madonna, a dying Foreign Legionnaire being rescued by an Arabian maiden, and so forth. In each studio, created and designated by the all-knowing Mme Irma, a web of fantasy has been woven around which the most solemn rituals and ceremonies are enacted. During those moments when Mme Irma's "visitors" live in their world of rapture, they dwell in ecstasy in a matriarchal sphere where Mme Irma, served by her priestesses, holds sway. For her sacred prostitutes, "she is a multiple womb, but in reality she remains herself, the one Goddess." Viewed unconsciously as a negative image by her men clients, Mme Irma and her brothel remain necessities for sexual fulfillment. They serve a function; they are instrumental in achieving a pragmatic goal.[9]

The spectators are told that only one function or role has not been asked for by a visitor—that of the Chief of Police. The Chief of Police (in real life Mme Irma's lover) represents the forces of reaction, the protector of the monarchy, the church, and the brothel. Such a role has not sufficiently stirred the imagination to bring about sexual fulfillment. There is nothing "sacred" or "religious" or "mythical" about the function of Chief of Police. Mme Irma declares: "The time's not ripe. My dear, your function isn't noble enough to offer dreamers an image that would enshrine them. Perhaps because it lacks illustrious ancestors? No, my dear fellow. . . . You have to resign yourself to the fact that your image does not yet conform to the liturgies of the brothel" (*B*, 44).

Meanwhile, Roger, the leader of the revolutionaries, the man who believes in pure, rational revolution and in the creation of an ideal state, declares his love for Chantal. Chantal was the only one of the prostitutes to flee Mme Irma's house of illusion because she could no longer stand playing the role of a mythical creature, incarnating an emblem, a collective image. She wanted to live in so-called reality. She has fallen in love with Roger, formerly a plumber, whom she met when he came to make repairs at the Grand Balcony. Near Roger and Chantal stand three revolutionaries with guns aimed at the Grand Balcony. They tell Roger that Chantal is needed for their cause. She must become their symbol or mascot and represent a sexual image of liberty, self-sacrifice, heroism. She must become a modern Joan of Arc and belong to the masses. If Chantal agrees, she will have given up one myth, which she had lived in Mme Irma's Grand Balcony, to adopt another. She accepts the new role and as she does so, she knows that she is not only giving up her lover, Roger, but her own life as well. She will now become a "singer on the barricades." The three revolutionists take her with them. Roger is now aware of the change that has come over Chantal: "It was to struggle against an image that Chantal became fixed in an image. The struggle no longer takes place in reality but in a closed field. . . . It is a struggle of allegories." Neither one side nor the other now sees the reasons for their revolt.

The revolution is progressing. The palace has been blown up, and the Queen and her court have been swept away. Only if the people can be made to believe that the symbols of monarchy are intact can the revolution be crushed. So, Mme Irma agrees, together with the Bishop, the General, and the Judge, to assume in reality the roles they play in her bordello.

Mme Irma prepares to dress up in the Queen's gown. She is going to live out her destiny as a Queen and bow to the crowd from her balcony. She, the Bishop, the General, the Judge, and the Hero (the Chief of Police) appear on the Balcony. Their appearance is sufficient to placate the crowd for the time being.

The revolution has been stamped out. Three photographers are waiting to photograph the three figures and the Queen in Mme Irma's bordello. The General, the Judge, and the Bishop who have now been thrust into the *real* world where their assumed functions carried them, must now exercise their power. They are timid and frightened at the thought of the demands that are going to be made upon them.

The photographers begin photographing the three figures in the typical positions required for popular consumption—the poses that symbolize their functions. The Bishop kneels and acts as though he were inundating the world with an image as he receives the sacrament. Since the photographer does not have a host handy, he borrows the Judge's monocle and uses it as a substitute. He puts it into the kneeling Bishop's mouth. The Judge will be photographed wearing a long face and the General posing as either Turenne, Bayard, or Wellington. As the Envoy puts it: "It's a true image, born of a false spectacle."

The Chief of Police arrives on the scene. Good news. The revolution is over. He is confident now that someone will choose his function. In this end he is having a gigantic mausoleum built for himself. It will, he is certain, attract somebody's fantasies and lend authority and stature to his profession. He wants to be supreme: "I want my image to be both legendary and supreme." A fitting symbol for his progression or function has been suggested to him: "I've been advised to appear in the form of a gigantic phallus." With such a symbol, the Chief of Police would be unique." "I shall be not the hundred-thousandth-reflection-within-a-reflection in a mirror, but the One and Only, into whom a hundred thousand want to merge" (*B,* 92, 96).

Mme Irma, beside herself with joy, announces that Roger, the leader of the defeated revolutionaries, has asked to impersonate the Chief of Police. They all watch Roger through Mme Irma's intricate television machinery. Roger has donned the *cothurni,* the padded shoulders, the rest of the Chief of Police's uniform, and he is being led by Carmen, one Mme Irma's prostitutes, down the road to immorality. He smokes a big cigar as he walks down the steps of the mausoleum. This mausoleum or "basilica of Lourdes or termite nest" was built for Roger, Carmen declares, by slaves whose great and only dream was to die for their hero. Roger is quickly reaching a state of ecstasy. The world takes on life, meaning, tone, and hue: "Everything breathes me and everything worships me! My history was lived so that a glorious page might be written and then read." Roger is now going to live out his new role to its very end. "I have the right to lead the character I have chosen to the very limit of his destiny . . . no, of mine . . . of merging his destiny with mine . . ." (*B,* 112). And in so saying, he turns his back to the audience and makes the gesture of castrating himself.

The real Chief of Police, who has watched this enactment through Mme Irma's machines, is delighted over the fate of his Image. He asks for enough food to last him for two thousand years and, in spite of Mme Irma's pleading, descends into the tomb he has constructed for himself and has himself immured. He has fulfilled his destiny now. He claims that he is stronger than the other three figures, that he reigns supreme: "I've won the right to go and sit and wait for two thousand years. You! Watch me live and die. For posterity. . . . I've won!" (*B,* 113).

A chatter of machine-gun fire is heard as a new revolution starts to break out. The three figures leave. Mme Irma turns out the lights and prepares her studios for the following day.

Dawn: the cry of the cock is heard. Mme Irma stops in the middle of the stage, faces the public and says: "You must now go home, where everything—you can be quite sure—will be even falser than here. . . . You must go now. You'll leave by the right, through the alley. . . . It's morning already." (*B,* 115).

Illusion versus Reality—Mask Identification

All in the Grand Balcony is sham. Even the Bishop's sacrilege is fantasy, for had his penitent really committed "deadly" sins, he would have to suffer the consequences. His revolt against reality exists only in his imagination. He is merely play-acting at it. Therefore, Mme Irma always sees to it that a false detail is added some place within the accessories or in the ritual that preludes each "visitor's" sexual act. Thus, the action that he is living out of his dream fantasy is not real. Reality must never break through because the "visitors' " enactments are exciting to them only if they are not authentic.[10]

But the world of illusion each being creates for himself is deceptive. The visitors know deep within themselves that it is false. Yet they persist in escaping into their world of fancy. They eventually wonder whether it is any more sham than life outside the brothel, where man persists in creating myths for himself in the form of the church, the magistrature, and the army. The Bishop, the Judge, and the General, who represent the aforementioned solid institutions, have acted upon the imaginations of people for centuries. The power that they wield is stressed by Genet theatrically, by means of the *cothurni* and padded shoulders the actors wear. Their size makes them superior to other human beings, as though they were standing on a balcony. These oversized men take the place of the gods, angels, heroes, and archcriminals Genet created in his novels (*Miracle of the Rose, Quarrel of Brest,* etc.). Genet needed the earlier figures at the time that he brought them out of limbo, as others need the institutions represented by the three figures. Such institutions stand for structure, authority, security—something "above" the people protecting them. Each institution is surrounded by its own set of codes, rituals, ceremonies, and symbols, which are powerful forces in keeping the people satisfied and in check. When such symbols prove to be ineffective, that is, no longer answer the needs of masses, they are overthrown and a whole new set is created.

The church, the law courts, and the army are man-made institutions that cannot function without man. The three figures on the Grand Balcony are therefore at once defiling and preserving these same institutions, because to fight something implies its existence. A Bishop needs a worshiper; a Judge, an offender; a General, a soldier. Each visitor as he enters Mme Irma's brothel chooses a subjectively significant role. The costumes and accessories he dons and the scenarios he creates give him the strength he lacks in ordinary life, where he has become "ineffective." By adopting the identity of another, he has, in effect, rejected his own. Such an action of self-rejection (also implicit in *The Maids* and in *Deathwatch*) is tantamount to an unconscious self-destruction or self-murder. In this respect, the men playing out the roles of Bishop,

Judge, and General are already psychologically dead or well on the way. Such psychological death has occurred (or will occur) because these men have become so identified with their vestments or masks, their scenarios, and the characters they have created for themselves, that they have become their own gods. As such they partake of their own myth, which they are unconsciously living out in the Grand Balcony.

These three figures, as a collective image, have lost all individuality. What once had been personal and individual has become collective. The Bishop is not an individual bishop, he is all the bishops wrapped into one. Were he an individual, he would have one and the same character with very little variation of attitude. Because of his complete identification with the attitude of the moment, he not only deludes himself but others around him. The mask he dons will correspond with his conscious intentions and will fit the environment he wants to create for himself. His "mask" frequently conceals the opposite unconscious attitude; that is, if the inflexible or unapproachable harsh mask were removed, it would reveal a dependent and susceptible inner personality, which has permitted its own destruction. It is no wonder, then, that the Bishop fears that the penitent may have committed "real" sins; or that the Judge claims that he would die were his verdicts "real"; or that the General has to hide his civilian clothes in order to play his part. The clothes they don, the personalities they enter into, are protective coverings that shield them from public view and hide what is personal and vulnerable. Their "masks" lend them authority and frequently longevity (in that they can live on eternally in these roles as parts of institutions that belong to the collective and the individual).

Roger, the idealist and revolutionary, wants to change the world and create a new one. He wants to annihilate the decayed, restrictive forces of the old regime, which had repressed new trends and developments. With the revolution new forces gush forth and sweep everything aside that might repress their expression. The clergy, the generals, the Queen—all have been done away with. And as this cleansing and transforming process takes place, the forces making it possible will need to create their own symbols and banners. The revolutionaries will fall into the same pitfalls as the monarchists. They will erect their own goddesses, perhaps to Reason, as they did during the French Revolution of 1789, and create their own heroes *à la* Robespierre, Marat, Danton, who in turn will spread blood and destruction all about while Mme Lafarge knits. Perhaps a Napoleon will arise from the cinders; perhaps a Commune from an occupation, as was the French experience in 1870. Monuments to heroes similar to Turenne, Bayard, Condé, and Wellington may be erected to new heroes who will have brought "salvation" to the world. Such men become gods and saviors because the multitudes have need of them at the time. Some men sacrifice their lives for an ideal; others give their blood. Genet's satire of the revolutionists and their myths is as devastating a commentary on humanity's idealism as Rabelais's sixteenth-century treatment on wars in his *Gargantua and Pantagruel*.

Roger discovers that he could not change the world. He can only create a "Reflection" of the "Image" he has conceived, which is based on the old world he has known. Roger is a visionary who loses out in his absolute, pure, and rational revolution. He learns why he had failed only after it is over. Man cannot live within the framework of reality (rational approach); he must be spurred on by some symbol-image or fantasy to realize his dream. Roger becomes ineffectual. His inability to change man's destiny or his own, his inability to act, his sense of inadequacy, all translated into moral terms, give rise to a sense of guilt that has to be expiated or punished by castration. When Roger castrates himself he destroys his productive, active, individual potential, which has already been symbolically destroyed with the failure of the revolution. His castration, then, is an admission of his impotence. It is a sacrifice of manly power that impels him into a state of regression and dependency.

Roger sacrifices his virility and can no longer dream of being the powerful revolutionary. He chooses to live out his destiny as the Chief of Police because such an image symbolizes power, physical strength, and authority, the very elements Roger lacks.

The Chief of Police, it is to be recalled, wants to reign supreme for two thousand years, which is comparable to the length of the reign of the Christian church. Once the Chief of Police comes upon his symbol—the phallus—and the nomenclature has been asked for, he stands more powerful than the Bishop, the Judge, or the General. He has become a man-god like Osiris, Dionysus, or Christ,[11] because, as he says, "Though my image be castrated in every brothel in the world, I remain intact. . . . An image of me will be perpetuated in secret. Mutilated? Yet a low Mass will be said to my glory. . . . Did you? Did you see me? There, just before, larger than large, stronger than strong, deader than dead (*B*, 112).

Like a man-god, the Chief of Police is castrated, yet he remains whole; he is divided, yet he remains one; he is entombed yet he lives.

He will be worshiped perhaps for two thousand years, as long as the food in his tomb lasts. Then the new religion he has brought, that of the phallus, will perhaps be overthrown and replaced by another "Reflection" of an "Image"—another myth and legend.

Mme Irma is wise. She knows more than Mme Lysiane (*Quarrel of Brest*) about human beings and their mysterious workings. She knows that within her quarters, illusion had become reality and the reality outside had become illusion. She is much more detached and stronger than Mme Lysiane. She can look upon the world with a cold eye—without illusions to blind her.

Mme Irma, like Lefranc of *Deathwatch,* comes to accept her fate. She has created a theater out of her house of illusions and has given an opportunity to live their fantasies, to those who cannot bear to face life's cruelties. Mme Irma, who looks upon life in a realistic manner, is no longer faceless. She sees her face—smudged and distorted as it may be, but at least it is a face and it lives.

Mme Irma and Lefrance represent in many ways the mature Genet, who is no longer the bellicose youth who idolized his heroes, who lost himself in his unrestrained and passionate worship of them, in his hatreds for society and institutions. He believes now that to destroy one institution is to see another rise in its place, no better, no worse. Life moves on. Another day brings more fantasies, more roles to be played over and over again in an absurd world where nothing is lasting or real, and where there is no meaning or purpose to anything.

Yet in *The Balcony* Genet seems to suggest that no matter how sordid, how painfully isolated man may feel, he goes on with his life. And Genet, like Mme Irma who prepares her house of illusions for the following day, will create his next scenario—*The Blacks*—in which the theme of illusion and reality will again be dramatized amid a more complex and ambiguous show of mirror images.

Chapter Ten
The Blacks

I tell you: one must still have chaos in one, to give birth to a dancing star. I tell you: you have still chaos in you.

—Friedrich Nietzsche, *Thus Spoke Zarathustra*

Les Nègres (*The Blacks*) was written in 1957 and performed for the first time in Paris on 28 October 1959 at the Théâtre de Lutèce. It was directed by Roger Blin and performed by an all-black troupe, Les Griots. This was the first production of a Genet play that won complete approval from the author.

The Blacks is a play within a play within a play, where actions and reactions are endlessly reflected; where murder, guilt, and expiation glisten in prismatic imagery. Hatred seems to be the motivating force of *The Blacks*. As Genet remarked: "What makes me feel so very close to them [blacks] is the hatred they bear for the white world; a hatred comparable to my own for the world that scorned me because I was a bastard, with no father and no mother."[1]

The Plot

The spectators witness the reenactment of the murder of a white woman supposedly perpetuated by a black. The murderer is then tried and judged by a White Court (blacks wearing white masks). The cantafalque on stage that is supposed to house the corpse is discovered to be empty and actually to be no catafalque at all, but rather four chairs covered with a white cloth. No body? No crime? The ritual murder supposedly enacted before the audience is, however, merely a cover up to draw the audience's attention away from the *real crime,* which has already been committed: a black man has rebelled against the whites, and his trial is taking place *off stage.* But the so-called real crime discovered by the audience is just as much of a sham as the one that is supposedly being enacted on stage. Is the offstage trial real, or does it occur only in the mind of the spectator? He is, after all, merely told of it and never witnesses it. And even if he did see it, would that make it genuine?

Or is *The Blacks* Pirandellian metatheater: simply a play within a play, theater about theater? While Pirandello's plays are metaphors for art as real and positive truth in contrast to the relativity and fluidity of life, for Genet these devices are weapons to be used to undermine stability, affirmations, and certainties. The multiple codes, messages, and variety of interactions used in *The Blacks,* which add to the already ambiguous, mystifying, and disturbing nature of the drama per se, are some of Genet's rather sinister subterfuges intended to exploit and affront people's insecurities.[2]

Nothing is *real* in *The Blacks* because all the action the audience witnesses occurs in a theater, a house of illusion where people seek entertainment and live and believe in the falsities they see. The whole ritual on stage, then, is a big joke, a game, "Clown Show," or "clownerie" (the subtitle of the play). Nothing is real, not even the emotions experienced by the actors or the spectators. Or are their feelings sincere? Were crimes really committed? Are the blacks acting out their hatreds? Are they trying to kill their white oppressors? Is it underdog against authority? Individual against society? Child against parent?

Spectator Participation

Just as Mme Irma's visitors played an intrinsic part in the action in the Grand Balcony, so the spectator becomes an active participant in *The Blacks.* In order to conjure effective audience reaction, Genet builts up a series of explosive emotions within the spectator. He insults his audience in an attempt to shake them, to destroy their complacency, to instill fear, guilt, and panic within their hearts just as they (society) instilled these feelings in his.

To further increase audience participation, Genet, paradoxically enough, has the actor shatter the empathy created between himself and the spectators by stepping out of character every now and then. By forcing such acute breaks in concentration, the onlooker becomes even more vulnerable. Tensions are thereby increased. As the black Archibald, a type of master of ceremonies in the play, says:

> But, in order that you may remain comfortably settled in your seats in the presence of the drama that is already unfolding here, in order that you be

assured that there is no danger of such a drama's worming its way into your precious lives, we shall even have the decency—a decency learned from you—to make communication impossible. We shall increase the distance that separates us—a distance that is basic—by our pomp, our manners, our insolence—for we are also actors. When my speech is over, everything here—here!—will take place in the delicate world of reprobation.[3]

Genet is a master-builder of shock and anguish. But, as Roger Blin explained:

If people are shocked by Genet's plays they are completely disarmed by his other great quality—his ability to evoke laughter, and laughter relieves the spectator. If a spectator is shocked by the obscenities he hears on stage, he is won over by the sheer beauty and poetry of Genet's language. Even those who feel they are being mocked and ridiculed are struck by the "truth" and burning sincerity of his poetry and are held by a sense of "fair-play."[4]

In order to mock and satirize the white spectators, and the whites in general, since they represent the forces of authority and oppression for him, Genet had to make certain that at least one white would be present at each performance. "Hatred" would be aimed at this one white, real or symbolic. In the second edition of *The Blacks,* Genet wrote:

This play, written, I repeat, by a white man, is intended for a white audience, but if, which is unlikely, it is ever performed before a black audience, then a white person, male or female, should be invited every evening. The organizer of the show should welcome him formally, dress him in ceremonial costume and lead him to his seat, preferably, in the front row of the orchestra. The actors will play for him. A spotlight should be focused upon this symbolic white throughout the performance.

But what if no white person accepted? Then let white masks be distributed to the black spectators as they enter the theatre. And if the blacks refuse the masks, then let a dummy be used. (*BL,* 4)

When Eugène Ionesco went to see *The Blacks* he took Genet's hatred, disguised as the hatred of blacks for whites, so personally, that he felt he was being attacked. He left the theater before the end of the performance. He sensed the great pleasure the Negro actors took in screaming out their hatred for the whites.

The Actors: Subjective and Objective Participation

The actors performing in *The Blacks* have an arduous task. During the first Parisian production, director Roger Blin was faced with serious problems. Some members of the cast were assimilated Negroes living in Paris. They were offended by Genet's language and by the fact that they were considered "savage" in the play. Yet the hatred of these "white" Negroes proved to be as violent, though hidden, as that of the African Negro: "One did not have to scratch too deeply to discover that they had suffered the tortures of racism and persecution, the immense pain of being considered inferior. Fundamentally, they agreed with every word in the play, with the spirit of the work."[5]

The first production held even further emotional appeal. It took place at a time when many African nations were seeking their independence. As Roger Blin said: "For these actors, then, the piece took on great meaning. Even the most assimilated Negro felt a deep craving for independence, to expel his oppressors.[6]

The nonprofessional actors hired to play in *The Blacks* discovered that they were not going to portray merely individual characters facing up to various situations in their lives, but many characters. They would act blacks playing at being blacks, that is, the whites' image of blacks. Frequently, they stepped out of these roles to become just Negro actors enacting other roles in the play within the play, or blacks seen through the eyes of other blacks. At other moments, they were blacks wearing white masks representing the image blacks have of the whites. They were forever playing mirror images, never seeing themselves through their own eyes, but through the eyes of others. They were, then, what Genet had become: the image society had made of him, the criminal he had turned himself into in order to fit society's image of him. As Village, one of the characters, points out, "We're like guilty prisoners who play at being guilty. . . ." This kind of acting, where an actor is called upon to portray different personalities and stages of psychological development, requires depth of feeling and understanding. It is no wonder, then, that Roger Blin spent two years training his cast.

Genet's Identification and Detachment with the Blacks

Genet wrote *The Blacks* for all Negroes the world over, from the mulatto to the blackest of Africans. It is an antiwhite play. It does not, however, glorify the blacks. Genet is under no illusions. He is not shedding any tears over the fate of the blacks, just as he would not over the fate of any minority or majority. If black society were supreme, it would be no different from white society. It would be, in fact, merely an image reflection of it. Unlike Brecht, Genet offers no paradise, no solutions, no answers. Genet paints a humanity with all its passions, hatreds, jealousies, and vices. He is trying to penetrate the surfaces of these beings, to understand them and himself, and so to liberate each in turn.

Genet identifies himself with the blacks because both are victims—pariahs in a (white) society. The blacks will live out their hatred for their white oppressors, and Genet, through them, will live out his for society and authority. For Genet, however, the years of solitude and degradation he had known in prison had their positive side. As Village says in *The Blacks,* "Slavery taught me dancing and singing." Without having experienced rejection, Genet might never have *sung,* meaning he might never have written. Without having known oppression, the blacks would never have wanted to rebel and destroy the oppressors. They would not have had the courage to rid Africa of the white colonizers and missionaries who had attempted, in many cases successfully, to eliminate what was individual to the so-called backward societies by molding their "savage" inhabitants in the white man's image. In *The Blacks* the tables are turned. The whites are killed, permitting the blacks to be released from their feelings of hatred through projection—at least in the theater. The whites in the audience are released from their feelings of hatred (fear and guilt) when the white-masked court judges and condemns the blacks for having killed a white woman, and when the black traitor is shot offstage.

Genet identifies himself with the blacks not only because both are rejected but because the color "black" to him (a white) represents his own dark, chthonic side. He fears this mysterious and unexplored aspect of himself, which he considers weak because it houses tenderness, nostalgia, and love for his fellowman. Yet, it will be through the very experiencing of his own shadow or dark side, his own shame and degradation, that he will be able to turn this negative force into a fruitful and positive life force. As Genet draws his dark aspect from within himself and exposes it to the light of consciousness before his audiences, he is able to face certain of his unconscious contents by projecting them on to the blacks. In Village's words: "I fear your sparkling darkness. Oh darkness, stately mother of my race, shadow, sheath that swathes me from top to toe, long sleep in which the frailest of your children would love to be shrouded, I know not whether you are beautiful, but you are Africa, oh monumental night, and I hate you. I hate you for filling my black eyes with sweetness. I hate you for making me thrust you from me, for making me hate you."[7]

The consummate artist that Genet now has become looks upon his creation in a detached manner. The emotional atmosphere of the play is controlled by Genet's wide variety of writing styles and techniques. Genet is as fertile as a swamp in the sun. He uses orchestrated laughter and weeping, the changing of vocal pitch, rhythmic dances, alternating speeds of line-reading between the white-masked court and the blacks, religious litanies, stylized gestures, lighting, and masks. In order to work his violence up to a peak, Genet not only repeats sounds, but lists words, hammering out the syllables and creating brutal, choppy, and contrapuntal effects by stressing consonants.

The Sets: An Intrinsic Part of the Drama

Just as the accessories and decors in *The Balcony* played a vital part in the drama, so do they in *The Blacks*. The stage sets for *The Blacks*, designed by André Acquart, are simple and symbolic. In the first production, they were made up of iron bars covered over by asbestos. The asbestos made the iron bars look more pliable. It was a stark and yet soft set. From the orchestra the decor looked like a giant sculpture. With proper manipulation of the lights, it assumed different shapes, different colors and moods. It reflected and participated in the action of the play.[8] The different levels on stage serve the same purpose as the *cothurni* and padded shoulders in *The Balcony*. The white court (blacks wearing white masks) standing on the higher ledge acquire a sense of authority, as well as an awareness of the precarious nature of its existence: To fall from the ledge (or balcony), thus giving up the position of authority, would mean death. The blacks standing on the stage (lower than the white court) experience a sense of inferiority and, at the same time, a more secure position, since they cannot fall from heights and are constantly in touch with the source of their energy, mother earth.

Flowers and a white cloth cover a catafalque placed in the center of the stage. The use of a white cloth indicates the beginning of a ceremony of opposites. Four blacks in tails and four black women in cheap-looking evening dresses dance to a Mozart minuet, thereby showing the incongruity of Western-imposed culture upon Africans. Archibald, who acts as the master of ceremonies, introduces his friends, whom, he says, are white, but have painted their faces with soot and spittle for tonight's performance. Felicity, Snow, Virtue, and Bobo are female characters; Village, Ville, and Diouf are males. Each member of the court sitting on the upper platform is a black wearing an incomplete white mask. Their costumes represent their social functions: the Queen, her Valet, the Governor, the Missionary, and the Judge. They have no personal names. They assume the personalities of their functions, as did the Bishop, the Judge, and the General in *The Balcony*. The court is interested in what is going on below, a mirror image of what takes place above. Here the blacks (Village, Virtue, Diouf, Bobo, and Snow) wear Western evening clothes and are directed by Archibald and Felicity. The ritual amid a burst of orchestrated laughter between both anagonistic groups, instills a primitive touch in the drama. Such rhythmic interchanges or tropes, as they could be called, are reminiscent of the medieval liturgical drama in France, when during a Christmas or Easter service two priests would speak a dialogue, or a priest and the choir would have a dialogue in a dramatization of the religious tableaux.

Illusion and Reality

The willed multiplicity and ambiguity so characteristic of Genet's works is carried to the extreme in *The Blacks*. Everything in this play is what the audience thinks it is or believes it to be. All is illusion, whether theatrical, optical, or emotional—even color is an illusion. And Genet asks: "What then is a Black? First of all, what's his color?" Since everything is relative, black can only exist if its opposite does. What is a black? A black is black to a white person. Whites are "pink or yellowish" to the blacks. Accompanying the white's conception of color are the values he gives to colors. In *The Balcony* each man identfies himself with his function or roles. The blacks living in a white country identify themselves with their color, which is the image the whites have of it. In al all-black country, black is invested with different values. In *The Blacks* (at the end), the white's conception of color is reversed. Black becomes the dominant color and represents the good and the pure, not evil, as it does in white-dominated countries. God is no longer white; white, not black, is the color of mourning in African countries: "To you, black was the color of priests and undertakers and orphans. But everything is changing. Whatever is gentle and kind and good and tender will be black. Milk will be black, sugar, rice, the sky, doves, hope, will be black" (*Bl,* 106).

The action of the play, Archibald tells the audience, is not going to be "pretty." It will take place in the world of "reprobation." Village is going to reenact his crime, the killing of a white woman. This act, symbolic of revolt and rebellion, must be performed as a secret rite, a mysterious ritual similar to those performed at Eleusis centuries before. In such fashion, each one present will experience catharsis, a release of his emotions of hate, aggression, and vindictiveness. Ville, it is decreed, must not be present. He becomes the liaison between the outside and inside worlds; he moves between the world of reality, where the real crime is being tried and judged, and the closed world of illusion, where the mock reenactment of mirror image takes place before the audience.

The interplay between illusion and reality will be carried still further when Village forces himself to reenact the excruciating act of revolt—the crime. He tells how he strangled a wine-soaked hag stretched out on a heap of rags. The Queen sheds a tear at this description. The missionary suggests a prayer to relieve tensions and to ask for pardon. Despite the asides, interruptions, excuses, and evasions that now go on between the blacks and the court—all in an effort to splinter whatever reality remains, even theatrical reality—Archibald insists the ritual continue. The blacks must be worthy of their "reprobation" and must bring the court to "pronounce the judgment which will condemn us." After all, it's only a game, a theatrical "clownerie," a play of reflecting images. "We'll play at being reflected in it, and we'll see ourselves—big black narcissists—slowly disappearing into its waters" (*Bl,* 38). The blacks see as many reflections and images of themselves as there are ripples in a lake after a stone is thrown into it: the image they have of the whites, the image they feel the whites have of them, the image the white audience has of them, the image they think the white audience has of them, and so forth. Such reflections, like many-faceted diamonds, again serve to abolish any kind of individual identity.

One might question the sincerity of the blacks. Are they sincere in demanding punishment? Are they sincere in pursuing the reenactment of their crime and later in pushing their rebellion against the whites forward? One might ask whether Quarrel was sincere when he called his homosexual relations with Nono a sacrifice. For some, the revolt will be sincere; for others, hypocritical. For many, the revolt will have actually occurred; for others, it lives only in their minds as a theatrical illusion. The purpose of this revolt (criminal deed) is important, however. It is to permit the blacks to emerge from their childlike state of infancy and dependency. The blacks must come to accept responsibilities, to be able to judge and face their acts. Only through punishment can the blacks experience expiation, the release of the guilt feelings induced by their sense of inadequacy and ineffectiveness. Judgment must then be followed by punishment.

The position of the court is as ambiguous as the question of sincerity. Such ambivalence is willed by Genet and is another example of the indeterminate relationships between everything in the cosmos: nothing is clear-cut, and things exist only by opposition. The court is made up of blacks wearing white masks. These masked beings secretly long to reverse the order of things and become the oppressors, the voice of authority. Yet, they know very well that they belong to the black, underprivileged race, just as the Bishop in *The Balcony* knows he is a gas man. There is one difference, however; when the Bishop has become a bishop in *real* life and carries out his duties and obligations, he becomes bored and anxious and refuses the job. The members of the White Court want to assume their obligations, which indicates a certain faith in the future. However, they do not want to assume their functions as whites, but as blacks. As the white Queen states at the end of the play, "We masked our faces in order to live the loathsome life of the Whites and at the same time to help you sink into shame, but our roles as actors are drawing to a close." The punitive position the blacks hold while playing the White Court places them in a superior position vis-à-vis their own brethren and serves to split them still further. Archibald sums up their ambiguous and false position when he says: "On this stage, we're like guilty prisoners who play at being guilty" (*Bl,* 114, 29).

The Ritual

The ritual murder performed by Village can be looked upon symbolically. It is an act of revolt against an oppressor. Sin, apostasy, revolt, rebellion, and disobedience, are all different forms of the same thing—emancipation or liberation from a previous attitude. The person indulging in this kind of act, if successfully accomplishing it, is released from the yoke or bondage of the dominating force. But every liberating act entails sacrifice and suffering, which in turn requires courage and fortitude. Revolt is an individual self-affirmation. Each new phase in individual autonomy is a step against a previous order of things. Expiation for a crime means the conscious realization of one's actions and the pain they entail. Battles for liberation are long and arduous and have been fought by many throughout the ages. Adam's revolt cost him paradise. Prometheus was doomed to hideous torture. Hippolytus rebelled against the "Great Mother" represented by Aphrodite; Perseus, against that represented by Medusa.[9]

For Genet, the "Great Mother" is the Queen: one white and one black:[10] The instrument of their destructive wills is their very duality. At the end of the play, the White Queen is killed and descends into the lower regions, or Hell, with the rest of her court. The Black Queen remains on stage and withdraws into darkness. That the Black Queen should return to dark, shadowy realms is not surprising, since she represents that mysterious aspect within Genet that worships the earthly side rooted in rich and nourishing soil as well as in slime and mud. The White Queen, since she now inhabits the lower regions, has met her chthonic counterpart, the Black Queen, who has withdrawn into that dimly lit realm, and now, symbolically, they have become one. Like the dual host mentioned in the play, which is colored white on one side and black on the other, both queens unite at the end of the drama and dwell in darkness, making their wills known only in mysterious ways.

There is another important ritual in the play not to be overlooked, that of incarnation. When Village reenacts his crime, he decides he needs a supernumerary. Diouf, the Black Vicar, must play the role of the white woman to be murdered. Diouf is, therefore, unmanned when he dons the white woman's mask and dress. He even says good-bye to his former life, to his "Great Black country."

The ritual or miracle of Incarnation now occurs. Virtue, the prostitute, kneels before Diouf. She recites the "Litany of the Livid," in a monocord tone, in the same manner as the "Litany of the Virgin" is recited, wrote Genet. The rhythms and sounds of the "Litany" and the homage paid to Diouf, first by Virtue and then by Snow and Bobo, are orchestrated in counterpoint to help effect the transformation. The process of transformation is taking place on stage as it does in the Mass. Diouf attempts to include the believer (congregation–theater audience) in his sacrifice. Diouf, the Virgin, is the sacrificial gift that must be given if expiation is to follow. An endeavor to create a "participation mystique" between Diouf (Virgin) and the congregation (blacks) is now apparent. The congregation's collective soul, it is hoped, will be assimilated into that of Diouf's. The transformation rite ends. Diouf has now experienced his death as a black vicar and his resurrection as a white woman.

Now, because Village has experienced a mystical union with Diouf-Virgin, he has the strength to go on. He lunges forward, hails Diouf-Virgin, and begins his sensual reenactment of what we now learn was the rape and strangulation of a white woman. Village is proud of his sensuality, of the desire he brings out in the white woman: "Listen to the singing of my thighs. . . ." His thighs fascinated her, he says. He tells of what happened when he went to see her: "So there I was, nestling in the shadow. And I whispered to her: Listen to the singing of my thighs! Listen. . . . That sound is the mewing of panthers and tigers. When they bend, that means leopards are stretching" (*Bl,* 64).

Diouf is three times transformed: first, as an actor; second, as a woman; third, as a procreating Virgin. From her (his) skirts now comes forth dolls representing the Governor, the Valet, the Judge, the Missionary, and the Queen. They are arranged to the left on the stage under the balcony where the court sits. These dolls are again mirror images of the court above and have been brought forth to add to the multiplicity of the action and its ritualistic aspect.

In order not to shock the overly prudish, the ritual murder will occur off stage. Village kills the white woman (Diouf) behind the scenes. Or does he?

In *The Blacks,* as in *The Balcony,* Genet takes to task decaying functions and organizations that make up society. In this play, the great figures are Missionary, Governor, Judge, Valet (merchant or soldier), and the Queen. There is no king or father principle in this society. The mother image in the form of a Queen reigns supreme in both black and white worlds. The Queen is kind and good, much in the same fashion as Mme Lysiane and Mme Irma. In this respect, one is reminded of the game of chess and the power the Queen wields there as opposed to the impotent King: "The collection would have been incomplete without the Mother. Tomorrow, and in the ceremonies to come you'll represent the Worthy Mother of the heroes who died thinking they'd killed us, but who were devoured by our fury and our black ants" (*Bl,* 124).

Chapter Eleven
The Screens

The virgin, the vivacious and the beautiful today
Shall it tear us with a drunken wing's blow
This hard forgotten lake haunted under the frost
The transparent glacier of flights that never were!

A swan of the past remembers that it is he
Magnificent but without hope of release
For not having sung of the region where life
When from sterile winter dazzled ennui.

His whole collar will shake this white agony
Inflicted by space on the bird who denies it,
But not the horror of earth where his plumage is caught.

Phantom whose pure brilliance is assigned this spot,
Immobilising himself in disdain's cold dream
Donned by the Swan in his useless exile.

—Stéphane Mallarmé,
The virgin, the vivacious and the beautiful today

Les Paravents (*The Screens*) is a play with seventeen scenes and ninety-six characters. Although inordinately long and complex, it is epic in dimension. Genet chose Blin to direct *The Screens,* which was produced in Paris in 1966 at the Théâtre de France (with the Madeleine Renaud and Jean-Louis Barrault Company). André Acquard was called upon to design the sets and create the costumes. He excelled in both areas: his sets were extraordinarily simple, thereby accentuating their impact. As for the costumes, Genet praised them in referring to them as only "an accouterment": because they did not really clothe the characters, they revealed their inner natures. Genet insisted that their makeup be "extremely violent," as well as "asymmetrical."[1] Summing up the infinite dimensionality of *The Screens,* Roger Blin said that the play was "a culmination of everything Genet has done. All his past themes have been woven into a solid network. It's like a modern tapestry with all its brilliant, flashing, discordant, and swiftly moving colors . . . a tapestry possessing both artistry and depth."[2]

Blin was correct in his assessment. Even in Genet's last, posthumous work, *A Captive in Love*—which deals with his travels to North Africa, focusing mainly on the Palestinians, their camp life, and guerrilla tactics—he never again wrote for the theater. Genet had said what he had to say in his great plays—among the greatest of the twentieth century and of all time. Like Rimbaud, who remained silent after his creative period, so the volcanic embers that had flamed forth in Genet and had been embedded in his works of art, had also cooled and transformed into ash.

The Screens introduces the spectators to an Arab village with its brothel, its colonists, police, judge, missionaries, and so forth. Genet sides, as far as his nature allows him any direct involvement, with the pariah—in this case, the Arabs. His identification with the Arabs does not, any more than did his identification with the blacks, mean that he idealizes them. Genet sides with the Arabs only insofar as they are the underdog attempting to overturn decayed colonial establishments and to infuse life into a new society, though a new society will in turn give rise to disorder, decay, and dissolution.

Genet paints a glowing picture of the cowed Arabs and their values, which are the opposite of those of the colonials. The Arabs (as the blacks before them) see themselves through the eyes of the colonials: they live in filth, surrounded by flies feeding on children's eyes and on rotting corpses; amorality is the order of the day; and degradation is part of the national heritage. Yet even the Arabs nourish illusions of overcoming the hated colonials, of stealing what rightfully belongs to them.

The Mother, the symbol of the matriarch, reigns supreme in *The Screens*. She will propel the march of the shadows on stage. She will direct and sweep them—particularly Saïd, her son, and Leila, his "saintly" wife. The Mother, by her very lack of a proper name, reveals her anonymity and her collective and transpersonal nature. She appears as a function, an archetype, rather than as a personal mother. She fulfills in this manner the need of encountering what has not been lived through, what Genet had never experienced—the mother. She will be a powerful figure throughout and as such will contrast dramatically with her outside vestments, a patched violet satin dress that she wears continuously. She is so "thin" that she seems almost to have no body at all—and exists almost as a shadow figure.

The various struggles between opposing forces, whether political, social, moral or literary, fuel Genet with energy. Genet thrives on tension. It ignites in him a kind of creative explosion. His writing is a struggle to express the inexpressible, to render the impalpable palpable, to make the infinite finite. Mallarmé's search for unity in the "word" that would express all sensations and associations failed and ended in sterility—the blank page. Genet's anguish is still positive and active.

His prose in *The Screen* is closer to his novels than to his plays. Less constrained, less dense, *The Screens* covers a broader field in an expanded universe, and like a fugue its themes repeat themselves on various levels and tones. Genet, as always, seeks to shock and provoke a reaction in the spectator. Through the use of extreme realism, insolence, and violence, he attempts to create an answering violence in the audience.

The theater has become Genet's battleground. *The Screens* is a weapon cast in society's face: it is Genet's call to arms. He seems to need living contact with his opponents (the audience) in order to find expression for his manifold complexities. They must stand on the stage in their skeletal forms before the multiplying floodlights, and fight and struggle against overwhelming odds, which society in the form of the audience represents.

The Plot

For the sake of clarity, I draw only a skeletal plot summary here. The rest of the chapter will deal with the separate themes involved in this extremely complex work: the brothel, judge-god, mourning, time, and death.

The Screens takes place in three stages: scenes 1–10 depict the social life of a small Algerian village prior to the outbreak of war; scenes 11–13 dramatize the conflict that has just broken out; and in scenes 14–17 the Algerian army is given machine-guns and uses them.

As the play opens, Saïd and his Mother are walking. It is hot. The sun is just about to rise on Saïd's new life. It is his wedding day. He sees and wants to see only sadness and grief about him. He is the poorest man for miles around, and he is to marry Leila, the ugliest girl. The Mother taunts her son. He must learn how to treat Leila as an ugly woman. "Vomit on her," she advises him. It is not easy to accept ugliness, but if he is to fulfill his destiny, he must carve the most difficult of paths for himself. Saïd looks at his mother and asks her to put on her high-heeled shoes. The skeletal, rag-dressed, filthy, spindle-legged hag dons her unmatched high-heeled shoes, a red one retrieved from a garbage heap and a white one found in a washroom. The grotesque has reached its culminating point. The Mother's power becomes manifest scenically because of these shoes, which give her height and a feeling of power and authority. She begins to dance for Saïd, and he is taken with her breathless beauty. "You're beautiful in them. Keep them on, and dance!"[3]

The dance is over, the Mother struggles with Saïd to pick up the valise, supposedly filled with wedding gifts for Saïd's and Leila's wedding. The valise falls, bursts open, and is revealed to be empty. Saïd and his Mother then roar with laughter. The emptiness of the suitcase implies that those things once considered valuable, the wedding presents within, are nonexistent. Other values must be sought and found. What are these values to be? Certainly not material possessions. The illusions Saïd and the Mother had nourished concerning these have proved to be void.

Saïd is an ascetic figure who renounces the world of the living in order to dwell in that of slime and abjection. He has set a task for himself: that of degradation, which costs him every conceivable joy. Leila worships the image she has of Saïd and, in order to be worthy of her ideal, tortures herself; she makes herself even uglier than she already is. Some critics have seen Leila as Saïd's feminine double: the metaphor of a male homosexual.

Saïd needs Leila's ugliness as a means of inflicting suffering upon himself. She becomes a vehicle for Saïd's ascetic ascension. Through her he will rub his nose in slime, will be put face to face with the sordid side of existence. Leila's ugliness will be characterized and exaggerated in all possible ways throughout the play in order to show Saïd's progression: the fulfillment of his destiny.

The first time the audience meets Leila, her face is covered with a black hood. She is alone, skipping around in a pair of Saïd's worn, patched trousers that are standing upright. She beckons them to approach, but they remain immobile. She walks toward them and speaks to them. They are "strolling about at night" in her dreams, she says. Saïd's trousers have become a fetish, a means of arousing emotions. Yet, like the suitcase, they are empty. The illusions she has had of Saïd and of her marital life with him are void, drained, as empty as a shell, a figment of her imagination. Yet it is these very illusions that permit her to go on living and fill the aching void that is her life. She is not yet strong enough to reach or fulfill her destiny, that is, to reach the extremes of ugliness, just as Saïd is not yet reach to achieve the depths of his degradation. Leila's initiation into horror will be difficult and painful, as will be Saïd's. She will bloom on cruelty and insults like those the Mother casts at her: "I tell you once and for all, and in plain language, because he won't dare. And he's not good-natured like me: you're hideous. Since you're ugly, be idiotic. And don't slobber" (*S*, 26). Hurt is heaped upon hurt. Leila squats while her mother-in-law and Saïd defame her. She begins to crawl out of the room like an animal. She is going, she says: "To wipe my nose in the garden, to wash away my snot and tears, and to comfort myself in the nettles" (*S*, 28). The extreme pain she undergoes and the sacrifice she experiences can find relief only when she withdraws into herself, her solitude. Alone in the garden, she communes, as Genet had once done, with the vegetable, mineral, and animal worlds. In those regions, not understandable to many, Leila, both outcast and rejected, finds needed comfort. Among the nettles, the coarse herbs armed with stinging hairs, amid injury, she will be crucified. Leila's unending masochism, like that of the ascetic saint in many cases, permits her to enjoy the torture she undergoes.

Shame is not sufficient. To dazzle with shame is Leila's intention. Leila is not only ugly, idiotic, a thief, a beggar, comments Saïd, but she has become a cripple besides. When exhaustion overcomes her in her travels with Saïd, she stops by the roadside and takes out her comb. Saïd grabs it and breaks it. He does not want her to become beautiful, but uglier. Her trial continues, and her sacrifice of the physical—so important to a woman—is her initiation ceremony into eternity.

> I'll obey you. But I want—it's my ugliness, earned hour by hour, that speaks or what speaks? I want you to stop looking backward. I want you to lead me without flinching to the land of the shadow and of the monster. I want you to plunge into irrevocable grief. I want you—it's my ugliness, earned minute by minute, that speaks—to be without hope. I want you to choose evil and always evil. I want you to know only hate and never love. I want you—it's my ugliness, earned second by second, that speaks—to refuse the brilliance of darkness, the softness of flint, and the honey of thistles. . . . We're here, and we're here, so that those who are sending us here realize that they're not here. (*S*, 108)

At the end of the play, Leila has but one eye. She has, therefore, reached her glory. She has become even uglier than she had imagined she could become. She has destroyed everything about her, together with herself, in order to be worthy of the "ascetic" Saïd.

When Saïd is questioned about his feelings for Leila, he tells of the difficulties involved in leading the life of an ascetic. Frequently, he almost succumbs to pity, because of his love for Leila: "I'm not saying I was never on the point of weakening, a tenderness, like the shadow of a leaf trembling above us, ready to alight, but I'd take hold of myself" (*S*, 190). As Leila's ugliness increases, so does Saïd's compassion, his love and admiration for her, which makes more difficult his task in this sadomasochistic round.

Leila and Saïd have learned to be solitary the hard way. Destroy within one's being every trace of beauty and pity, of sympathy for others and for oneself; wreck those who love you and who are attracted to you; live alone, in a prison cell or on a mountaintop, and when a world of timelessness and spacelessness, of extreme solitude has been attained, when the rational no longer limits one's horizons, then *another world* (that of the dead) will come into existence.

In addition to the central plot, the images of the Mother, Saïd, and Leila, two other actions take place in *The Screens:* the war being fought between the Arabs and the colonials, or the exploited and exploiters; and the life at the brothel. These two aspects of *The Screens* are analyzed below.

The Sets

The decor that figures as a character in this four-and-a-half-hour spectacle is described by Roger Blin: "the sets will be made up of numerous screens which will be brought on stage from the left, from the right, and from the back. The screens will be placed on three different levels. Their appearance and disappearance on stage will blend with the general tempo of the piece. They will be part of the play, while being dramatic entities unto themselves."[4] Just as the *cothurni* and padded shoulders were used in *The Balcony* to represent authority and prestige and the iron bars wrapped in asbestos were used in *The Blacks* to symbolize social rank and power, so gradations in the levels of the screens on stage serve to express social differences in both the living and the dead societies, the conscious and unconscious realms. On the screens will be drawn stage accessories indicating the placement of the scene—a palm tree or a tombstone, for example. The Arabs will draw the progress of their revolt, which is taking place behind the scenes, on the screens. Insofar as these drawings are means of indicating action unseen by the spectator, the screens tell a story and replace in some respects the Greek chorus. The screens perform yet another function: they draw a dramatic line or demarcation between the visible and invisible, death and life, conscious and unconscious, dream and reality.

The lighting effects also play their part. In some areas or levels on stage the screens are lit up either simultaneously or separately; in other places there is darkness. Such changes in light and darkness imply the march of consciousness through the various levels of the unconscious: life through death. A very wide gradation in values is then measured by the degree of brilliance shining on the screens.

There are still other functions for the accessories, mentioned by the author. Real objects, at least one for each scene, are to be placed on stage to contrast more violently with the *trompe-l'oeil* objects painted on the screens. Each protagonist, it is further stated, will be masked or highly made up and will wear a false nose or chin. Such exteriors will pave the way for the inward march, which is the play.

The Theme of the Brothel

The theme of the brothel already treated by Genet in *Quarrel of Brest* and in *The Balcony* is again introduced into *The Screens* as an additional means of earning degradation. Warda, the queen of the prostitutes in *The Screens,* is forty years old. Her buck teeth, with lots of gold on them, are false. She wears a heavy gold lamé dress, high-heeled shoes, a chignon, a long, thin, false nose, bracelets, a tiara, and heavy makeup. As Genet caricatures ugliness, so he caricatures beauty by pushing it to its limits. The excessive garb serves as Warda's mask just as the black hood, the high heels, and the ragged costumes hide Leila, the Mother, and Saïd from public view.

Warda, in Genet's words, is a total "ruin" who should provoke a taste of cinders in the spectators mouth and a smell of rot in his nose (*L,* 16). Warda in certain respects is like Mme Lysiane and Mme Irma, but even more regal. The ritual in *The Screens* begins as Warda is being made up and dressed; she picks her teeth with a long, gold hatpin. Warda enjoys the ceremony of the donning of her vestments; the exchange of one life for another, as the Bishop, the General, and the Judge reveled each time they put on their costumes in *The Balcony.*

It has taken toil on Warda's part to achieve her ideal, the image she had envisioned for herself. In order for such a transformation to occur, she has had to destroy her true being, which was weak, nostalgic, and incapable of the slightest action. "A whore's not something you can improvise. She has to ripen. It took me twenty-four years. And I'm gifted." Mme Lysiane had not hardened sufficiently. Mme Irma faced her reality but did not perfect it; she did not turn her function into a work of art. Warda has reached the pinnacle. She has succeeded in completely divesting herself of her original nature. What remains of her original self beneath her new personality as represented by her clothes? "My outfits! Underneath, there's not much left . . ." (*S,* 19, 22). Like the suitcase or the pants, she is an empty shell.

In the bordello, "Mass is being said," to quote Roger Blin's words, and "a very sacred Mass." It is during this period that one experiences communion with the divine, one is initiated into the mysteries of the mask-begetting ceremony. Mask-begetting requires sacrifice, suicide, in order to experience resurrection, that is, rebirth. Genet's vocabulary, consequently, is constellated with such words as death, hatred, fire, darkness, sun, and treasure.

Warda's attempt at self-destruction has never really been successful. In fact, she sometimes comes to resent the crushing task she has imposed upon herself and which she has failed to accomplish fully until now. She nourishes illusions of success, of turning herself into a statue of perfection, of being totally detached and unfeeling in all of her relationships, of resembling Astarte, who was so ruthless and savage in her relations with men. She wants to be despised and feel nothing: "Mirror, mirror, where is the time when I could stare at myself and yawn, for hours on end? There was a great distance, there was a Sahara Desert, between me, Warda, and the most despised woman of the village, between me and Leila (*S,* 139).

During the Arab-colonial war, Warda gains acceptance from the bourgeois grocer and butcher. She is no longer that complete and absolute pariah she longs to be. Unlike Leila, she no longer enjoys the solitude that had become her grandeur. She must, therefore, take events into her own hands. She must regain the status she believes she has lost. She must die. She chooses crucifixion as her mode of initiation, the most grueling of experiences, so that she can earn her martyrdom and saintliness. Warda's supreme ascetic act of strength, her crucifixion, is played out with hat pins and knitting needles instead of nails. Six women who are knitting swoop down upon Warda like hornets. They pounced "on the flower and pierced the skin of its belly and neck." Like the flies who feed on corpses, so the hornet-knitters sting and sink deep like nails into Warda's flesh. Genet implies that Warda has, like Christ, taken the sins of the world upon herself. She has known all of them, as did St. Mary the Egyptian, who prostituted her way to Jerusalem.

Warda has now experienced such anguish and pain as will place her above others. Her crucifixion is her initiation into the *other realm.* She hails her own death. It is the culmination of her life. She has turned herself into her own mask, an inhuman statue, a hollow object, a dress with no inside. Death now places her beyond life, in the world beyond the screens on stage, in that transpersonal realm.

The Theme of War

Genet's colonist is a villain. He heaps ridicule on the conqueror: on Sir Harold, preoccupied with the "orange grove" for which he would sacrifice anything; on Mr. Blankensee, who loves his roses and is obsessed by them to the extent that their very existence gives him a reason for living. Both the orange and the rose are used with satiric intent. They are symbolic elements necessary for survival.

Sir Harold, who loves his orange grove, reminds one of the General in *The Balcony* in that both are sexually attracted to their horses. As Sir Harold leaves the stage with his animal, he leaves a fetish, a glove, in his place, so that the workmen, Saïd among them, will continue their toil: "A wonderful pigskin glove flies in, directed by a mechanism behind the screen. It remains in the air, as if suspended, in the center of stage." The glove symbolizes the colonialist—his grasping, guarding, ruthless side. But there is no hand in the glove. It is as empty as the valise, the pants, and the vestments.

The caricature of Mr. Blankensee is even more hostile. He has given names to his precious roses, and at night he attaches a bell to each of his rose bushes so that he can recognize them by their odor and sound: "My roses! With their strong, hard, triangular thorns on stems as stern as guardsmen at attention." For Genet the rose represents not only the spiritual and feeling aspects of man, but also the convict, the thorn, the hurtful side. What Mr. Blankensee is expressing is his love for nature's dualism: the rose is a reflection of its beauty and ugliness, its pleasure and pain.

The ceremony of war ranks high in Genet's list of rituals. As Mr. Blankensee and Sir Harold are conversing on the set, Arabs crawl about it and begin drawing flames on the screens, blowing on these flames until all the orange trees painted on the screens seem to grow. Loud, cracking sounds made behind the scenes make the spectacle even more dazzling. But both men are so absorbed in their discussion that they remain unaware of the signs of deep unrest and discontent stirring about them.

As war begins, the Soldiers, the Sergeant, the Lieutenant, and the Legionnaires appear, all modeled on Genet's earlier soldier-characters: Riton, Erik, and the General. As the Lieutenant in *The Screens* is handed his uniform, one item at a time, a mask-begetting ritual begins as it did in *The Balcony,* when the General was given his vestments. When the Lieutenant is fully dressed in uniform, he is capable of every demand made upon him, just as Warda and so many other of Genet's earlier characters had been. The Lieutenant has gained strength in authority and power through his uniform and can how expound on the glories of warfare.

Other military ceremonies take place in *The Screens.* A tall dummy covered from top to bottom with all kinds of decorations is placed on a platform. Beside it, a woman perches on a chair and pins decorations on the dummy's shoulder. Near the chair is an old gentleman carrying a cushion, to which are pinned thirty or forty different kinds of medals.

A contrasting ceremony takes place in the Arab camp. There the Arabs are drawing on the screens monstrously enlarged revolvers, bloodstains, screaming mouths, a heart, a house in flames, four feet, heads, hands, guns. Death is all about. The stronger the hatred, the greater the war.

It is not always easy to provoke a war, to force evil to prevail. In order to be able to heighten one's crimes, to achieve the limit in evil, one must call on God, for God alone possesses the dual powers of good and evil in one: "Thank you, father. Get God in on it. Let him commit his crimes right and left, let him kill, let him pulverize, let him destroy. Go. Write your prayer on the wall. If you can't find any more crimes, steal crimes from heaven, it's bursting with them! Wangle the murders of the gods, their rapes, their fires, their incest, their lies, their butcheries! Wangle them and bring them! There! As for the women, let them give birth to monsters!" (*S,* 102). Man, bound by his rational concepts, is incapable of limitless vision and so is unable to perpetuate the greatest of crimes. Only God, the omniscient, can bring about a state of perfect evil unimaginable to mortal man.

The Theme of the Judge—God

Genet does not neglect the Judge, the Cadi, as he is called in Arab countries, in *The Screens.* The Judge as a collective figure has been dealt with in the *Miracle of the Rose, The Balcony,* and *The Blacks,* among other works. In *The Screens* the Judge pronounces a verdict on a Flute Player who has been hauled into court by the Gendarme for begging. The Flute Player, we learn, has spend two years learning how to play the flute through his nose. He did not put himself through such a rigorous training period for the beauty of sound that might result, but rather to surpass or overcome the difficulty of his endeavor. Here, then, is another example of Genet's characters trying to "overcome," trying to deprive themselves of joy and perhaps in so doing to experience another kind of satisfaction. The Judge exonerates the Flute Player.

After hearing several cases, the Judge laments over the fact that God has left him. He therefore feels incapable of rendering any verdict. He has lost his inspiration, his principles, his codes, his ethics—all have vanished. When Saïd enters and insists upon being sentenced for theft, the Judge refuses, though he understands Saïd's inner necessity for punishment. The Judge wants to deny Saïd the pleasure of torturing himself. Let Saïd "wallow" in a constant state of despair, for to heighten his suffering by judging him would lead to his happiness—a state that would negate his wanted despair and would render his masochism or asceticism of no value.

Furthermore, now that the divine spirit no longer inhabits the Cadi, he no longer knows the right answers. Are there answers? Are there principles? His situation as Judge appears "nonsensical." He says: "I'm judge of a village where ghastly crimes are probably committed every minute—or is anything a crime." He is sure of nothing anymore because he discovers that everything is relative. To be a criminal in Nazi Germany did not make one stand out, since that country was a land of criminals. To kill in France, however, was considered a crime. If an Arab steals, he has not changed, he is an Arab. If a Frenchman robs, he is a thief. There are no truths, nor are there true values. The code established in each society is different and follows the dictates of the group as a whole.

Saïd insists upon punishment. His masochism can only be glorified through punishment. His pain must be increased to pay for the guilt of being alive. Saïd declares that he is not asking "that God go to the trouble of opening a prison door for me. A Cadi can do it." By the same token, if a cadi (an Arab judge) can dispense law, then there is no need for a higher law which transcends the limitations of human understanding. No need for God. Either one or the other—judge or God. "Either God judges you—he knows all, but he's no longer here—or else you judge yourself and I serve no purpose" (*S,* 51).

To select a judge is to deny man's function and responsibilities to himself and to others. To judge oneself, however, is the most difficult task. If one succeeds in this endeavor, then one assumes the role of God. Man is his own master, for he becomes God and judge at once. His inner god becomes his spiritual half, which acts as both his inspiration and rational self. To set up a human delegate from God is to remove man's responsibilities for himself. The human delegate is a buffer, a blind, and a fetish, implying that man is unequal to the task of carving out his future for himself. What would be accomplished by judging Saïd, questions the Cadi. He steals so frequently that the Cadi would be spending all of his time sending Saïd to jail. Acquittal would kill Saïd, who can thrive only on martyrdom, in the sordid, criminal world in which he lives and where he is constantly being condemned and rejected. Pardon and kindness would destroy the "glorious" image he has created of himself. Saïd, then, is a negative figure standing against all established order, and he will ascend to greatness in this area. For each new sortie into degradation, Saïd adds to his castle, stone by stone, as Leila pursued her ugliness and Warda her perfection in whoredom.

The Mourners

Mourning is another ritual Genet examines closely in *The Screens.* It is a ceremony that helps release one's distraught emotions and energies. Genet sees mourning, this "giving into oneself" as "pitiable," as another indication of weakness. The mourning ceremony, or the mockery of it, must therefore be performed only by people who are not emotionally attached to the deceased. For this reason, the dead Si Slimane, Saïd's father, has forbidden his wife, Saïd's mother, from mourning him. The professional mourners, however, wearing black veils, rush to the burial ground screeching: "Hurry up! If we're late, there'll be no flies left! The flies. The flies! The flies!" (*S,* 40). The women discourse on the flies, the incessant running and crawling of these insects all about in cellars, ceilings, the skin, the food, the dead, and decayed.

The flies represent the revolting, sordid, gluey, unwanted aspects of man that come to plague him. They are a scourge and a parasite, feeding continuously on blood and death. Yet these very insects, as rejects, like some humans, are in need of kindness to fill the void about them. In *The Screens,* the flies become a mirror image of the mourners, like a black swarm coming to pay its respects to the departing corpse, feeding on it as did the harpies of old.

Kadidja, one of the mourners, is stripped, as we shall see, of all conventional assumptions. In Genet's words: "Her face purple, almost black. The color of Negroes' lips, more or less. Her wrinkles, which are numerous, will be white. I think they ought to start at the wings of her nose and move toward the hair, the ears, and the chin. Her hands, her lower arms, and her legs, made-up the same way" (*L,* 32). She is, then, both sign and symbol; a violation of eschatological time and space, living as she does in the beyond. She understands more deeply than the others the meaning of life and death.

Like Kadidja, the Mother of Saïd also understands death and eternity. She is already aware of the continuity of action when Saïd is first accused of theft and is taken to prison. When the accuser withdraws his charges, the Mother cries: "Your complaints are complaints for all eternity. . . ." The scar of accusation will not only remain, but as the years go by, will become imbedded more deeply in the flesh. What is there to do to remedy this situation? The accuser's solution is for the thief to hurls insults back at the accuser. Such action, the Mother retorts, is not easy.

> Not so easy. A just insult can take your breath away, can pluck your tongue out, can dim your sight. What do you do then? I know—dazzle them with my shame. Ah, if I were Saïd . . ." (*S,* 36).

When the Mother visits the grave of her husband Si Slimane, who has been killed fighting the *colons,* the ceremony of life and death begins. The Mother asks an old man to play the part of the Mouth. It will be through him, the intermediary between the living and the dead, that communication will take place. The Mouth has now simply materialized as if at a seance: one part matter and one part spirit. Si Slimane, the dead man, will enter the world of matter or the world of the living through the Mouth. He describes his feelings as the transformation takes place: "Despite the weight of the earth, I feel much lighter. I'm about to evaporate—it's a good thing you didn't wait and that you came this evening—all my juice is seeping into the veins of the cork trees and the heads of lettuce. I'm wandering through my land, and you, I merge with everyone else" (*S*, 55).

The Mother resents the fact that the official mourners, the Women in Black, chased her away from her husband's grave and forbade her to wail. Denied even the release that mourning would have brought her, jeered by the Mourners, the Mother remains totally alone. Such punishment has to be dealt to her, for she has become "puffed with pride": pride that her son is a thief and her daughter-in-law the ugliest girl around. Not everyone can boast of such heights in degradation. She will, however, have to learn to curb her pride and the joy she takes in her accomplishments, otherwise, even the dead will cast her out: "The dead, to be sure, are the last resort. The living spit in your face, but the dead envelop you in their big black, or white, wings. And protected by the wings, you could flout those who go afoot? But those who walk by the earth will be inside it before long. They're the shame. . . . Your pride cuts you off from the living, it won't win you the love of the dead. We're the official bondsmen for the living" (*S*, 57).

The Theme of Death

What is death as revealed in *The Screens*? As the colonial war continues and the participants fall under the bullets, one after the other, the audience meets them again in the realm of the dead. To enter the realm of the dead each figure appears behind a screen, then breaks through the screen's paper. After penetrating the land of the dead, each makes the same remark: "And they make such a fuss about it!" Those already dead and on a lower level of the stage, *lower* their heads to look at the newly dead entering from *above*. Such an effect indicates man's sightlessness and the unimportance of his outer eye; the prime mover is his inner eye, which lives within his body and sees from every pore and every position.

To break through the screens is the culmination of an initiation ritual. It is like the stripping away of all outer garments and penetrating the inner eye: "She's peeling off reason so as to arrive pure and like you to know the relationships between space and running, and the names of flies . . ." (*S*, 147). To strip away does not only mean to rid oneself of the material elements in life, but also of all the soft, flabby, and sentimental attitudes. Giacometti had performed this same feat, or this same ascetic act, when creating his statues: they, too, were bone hard.

In Genet's world of the dead there is "no time before," nor is there "time afterward." It is a world where eternal atemporal values live, unlimited by the categories of time and space imposed upon man by his conscious and rational being. In Genet's world of the dead, there are no memories of sins or goodness, either past, present, or future. Complete life or complete death is the *now,* a conception that cannot be explained in finite terms. As Si Slimane, a dead revolutionary, says in *The Screens,* "Time passes less and less. . . ." "Time does nothing either . . . ," the dead guard declares, "And standing to the end of time," "Kadidja exclaims, "There's no afterwards if there's no more time. . . . And when the General dies, the Lieutenant drags him away and says "and may the General roll down the depths of time." The characters in *The Screens* do not die. They become "unreal" beings, two-dimensional and opposed to the sense world of three-dimensional reality. These dead people are in the world of ideas, unaffected by conventional limitations such as time and space or temporal sensations or feelings.

Having once pierced through the screens, the barriers separating life from death, the conscious from the unconscious, or reality for illusion, the dead witness the actions of the living and comment on them in terms of eternity. They discuss the emblems man has set up for himself, his false goals and gods, the illusions in which he is forever ensnared, and the relativity of his judgments, values, and laws.

After Saïd's death during the Arab-colonial war, he is considered a hero in the world of the living. He wonders, however, how he will be judged in the world of the dead. He is told that in death "There are no more judges, there are only thieves, murderers, fire-brands. . . ." No one can judge Saïd because "no one has gone as far as you. . . ." How can another being dare to judge his fellowman if he has not experienced as strongly, as powerfully, as ascetically as Saïd. Unable to judge, to assess Saïd objectively, the dead, like the living, come to admire him. He merges "larger than life. . . . Your brow in the nebulae and your feet on the ocean. . . ." The dead tell him he will stand there huge and unique, till the end of time, that his voice will be like a "hundred thousand trumpets," that he will surpass his own weight. He becomes the Alpha and the Omega, the beginning and the end of everything.

Death is made in the image of life as man is made in the image of God. Death for Genet is an initiation into another type or phase of existence, which is a mirror image of the one that man knows on earth. To overcome the fear of death is to discover its secrets. Death is man's supreme test, his greatest act. To master death is to master life. To master both is to master the cosmos. Each time a character breaks through the screens he breaks through from one world to another, breaching the line between life and death, illusion and reality, the material and spiritual. Death for Genet is also the theater: "If we maintain that life and the stage are opposites, it is because we strongly suspect that the stage is a site closely akin to death, a place where all liberties are possible" (*S,* 12).

Saïd has fulfilled his destiny. He has become a legend, like the Angel of Revelation who made known to John a new heaven and earth. Saïd has renounced life. He has destroyed any kind of value or consciousness within himself. He has destroyed his individuality and become an object of worship, not only for Leila, but for the world at large. As such, he has entered into the collective image. He has become a legend or a myth just as the Chief of Police did in *The Balcony*.

Others in *The Screens* will stand for other forms of subversion that will come into their own now that a new Algerian nation has been born. The continuous blendings of realistic social views and images with Genet's poetic and theatrical use of the stage blurs the finality of political assessment or conclusive view on the critics' part. Opposition and confrontation are the lot of all nations and governments. Subversion and exploitation of the oppressed will always come to pass. Stasis encourages decadence. Such have been the lessons of history.

Yet Genet says that the Saïd story was necessary, as are all stories with a "moral" that recount man's greatness, his asceticism, and his insight. In such anguish, man reaches the most profound level of his being and sings his soul as it splinters forth. It is through such experiences, which provoke the artistic creation, that one gains eternity and conquers death. The word, solitary and stripped of its essence like a Giacometti statue, takes on life when infused with the spirit of its creator. The energy that causes the release of the word or the song (artistic creation) is the same energy that drove Genet to seek eternity in the collective drama.

Conclusion

Jean Genet, the orphan, the homosexual, the criminal, not only *traversed* life's land, but groveled in it and ate of it. Thrown entirely upon his own resources as early as he could remember, he developed a rich inner existence that he felt compelled to expel. His energies and fire burst forth in the form of perverted sexuality and destructive aggressive acts. Such negative activities, however, did not seem to fulfill Genet's emotional or artistic needs. A more positive outlet had to be found.

From 1942 to 1949, Genet wrote frenetically, transforming the base metal that was his life into the works of art that are his books. He experienced life deeply, and the themes he treated were universal. After 1949 Genet wrote mostly for the theater, synthesizing, tightening, and sounding out both his prose and his views. Though Genet, the "fighter" and the "destroyer," was ever-present, the society he had formerly wanted to crush he now accepted for what it was. He saw society as a composite of beings, hopelessly embroiled in their own sordid and petty natures. Fearing to face their smudged souls, they created a world of illusion into which they forever sought escape in a vain attempt to experience some semblance of joy. And the dance macabre that life represents, continues into death, its mirror image.

Man's *raison d'être,* according to Genet, is his artistic creation, which is a palpable expression of self, the eternal within man. It is through the self, as it is manifested in the work of art, that each sensitive individual can come to understand, feel, and recognize certain aspects of himself in his fellow human beings—be they modern or ancient. During these moments of awareness or of empathy between subject and object, the veil of solitude that cloaks each being vanishes and the burden of loneliness becomes a little less difficult to bear.

That Genet's attitudes are considered base, sordid, perverted, and nihilistic by many is not really the question. Genet lived out his life as best suited him. His credo evolved from his subjective experience. His work ranks with the greatest of the century. Genet was a literary phenomenon.

If audiences and readers take Genet's message lightly; if they try to emulate his ways instead of struggling to work out their own; if they use him to create a new and giddy fad—they will be as guilty of vice as any murderer is. If, on the other hand, they take Genet's brand of humanity seriously and subsequently take stock of themselves, they can increase their understanding of themselves by sounding out their own souls, honestly and courageously, rather than by merely glossing over surfaces. If readers take this approach to Genet, then his negativism will have been transformed into a fruitful and positive force.

Notes and References

Chapter One

1. *The Thief's Journal,* trans. Bernard Frenchtman (New York: Grove Press, 1964), 45; hereafter cited in the text as *TJ.*

2. Michel Foucault, *Discipline and Punish: The Birth of the Prison,* trans. Alan Sheridan (New York: Vintage Books, 1977), 292–96.

3. Edmund Bergler, *Homosexuality: Disease or Way of Life* (New York: Hill & Wang, 1956), 80.

4. Richard N. Coe, ed., *The Theater of Jean Genet: A Casebook* (New York: Grove Press, 1970), 20–30.

5. Ibid.

6. Jean-Paul Sartre, *Saint Genet, comédien et martyr* (Paris: Gallimard, 1951), 144.

7. "Interview with Jean Genet," *Playboy Magazine,* April 1964, 45–53; hereafter cited in the text as *I.*

8. Sartre, *Saint Genet,* 460.

9. Harry E. Stewart, "Capefigue: An Historical Source for Jean Genet's Fantasies," *Romance Notes* 22 (Spring 1982):254–58.

10. Robert Wilcocks, "Genet's Preoccupation with Language," *Modern Language Review* 65 (October 1970):786–92.

11. Sartre, *Saint Genet,* 585.

12. Mohamed Choukri, *Jean Genet in Tangier* (New York: Ecco Press, 1974), 44–46.

13. Ibid., 46, 54, 56.

14. Ibid., 59, 49.

15. Bettina L. Knapp, "Interview with Roger Blin," *Tulane Drama Review* (Spring 1963):111–26.

16. *Un Captif amoureux* (Paris: Gallimard, 1964), 205.

Chapter Two

1. Notre-Dame-des-Fleurs (Lyons: l'Arbalète, 1943); rev. ed. (Paris: Gallimard, 1951); hereafter the 1951 edition cited in the text as *OL.*

2. Tzetan Todorov, *Poétique* (Paris: Seuil, 1968), 52.

3. Camille Naish, *A Genetic Approach to Structures in the Work of Jean Genet* (Cambridge, Mass.: Harvard University Press, 1978), 63.

4. Mary Ann Frese Witt, "Spatial Narration in Jean Genet's *Notre Dame des Fleurs* and *Le Balcon,*" in *Myths and Realities of Contemporary French Theater: Comparative Views* (Lubbock: Texas Tech Press, 1985), 129.

5. Jean-Paul Sartre, foreword to *Our Lady of the Flowers,* trans. Bernard Frechtman (New York: Grove, 1964), 2.

6. Genet refers to "children," but they are really boys in their teens.

7. Arthur Rimbaud wrote, "Car Je est un autre" (Rimbaud to Paul Demeny, 15 May 1871; in *Oeuvres complètes* [Paris: Gallimard, 1954], 270).

8. L. A. C. Dobrez, *The Existential and Its Exits* (New York: St. Martin's Press, 1986), 223.

9. Jung posits that an oceanic phenomenon known as the collective unconscious or the objective psyche dwells at the bottom of the human psyche. The collective unconscious is common to all human beings and is cumulative throughout the ages. It consists of everything that is unknown as well as archetypes. Jung wrote: "The concept of the archetype is derived from the repeated observation that, for instance, the myth and fairy-tales of world literature contain definite motifs which crop up everywhere. We meet these same motifs in the fantasies, dreams, deliria, and delusions of individuals living today. These typical images and associations are what I call archetypal ideas. . . . The more vivid they are, the more they will be coloured by particularly strong feeling tones. . . . They impress, influence, and fascinate us. They have their origin in the archetype, which in itself is an irrepresentable unconscious, pre-existent form that seems to be part of the inherited structure of the psyche and can therefore manifest itself spontaneously anywhere, at any time. Because of its instinctual nature, the archetype underlies the feeling-toned complexes (q.v.) and shares their autonomy" (*Collected Works,* vol. 10 [New York: Pantheon Books, 1964], 229–30).

10. Victor Magnien, *Les Mystères d'Eleusis* (Paris, 1950), 45.

11. See Jung, *Collected Works,* vol. 12 (London: Routledge & Kegan Paul, 1953), 74.

12. C. Kerenyi, *The Gods of the Greeks* (New York: Grove Press, 1960), 139–40.

13. Jacques Derrida, *Glas,* trans. John P. Leavy, Jr., and Richard Rand (Lincoln: University of Nebraska Press, 1984), 28.

14. Kate Millet, "The Balance of Power," *Partisan Review,* no. 2 (1970):200.

15. Such a moral was plainly illustrated in the medieval miracle play *The Juggler of Our Lady.*

16. The Chimera was a terrible monster, a strange mixture of many beasts. Its body was part lion and part goat, its hind legs those of a dragon, its breath was fire. It lived in Lycia and caused great damage and was finally killed by Bellerophon.

17. The Griffin was a monster with the body of a lion, the head and wings of an eagle, its back covered with feathers. Like birds, it built its nest, but instead of an egg it laid an agate. It had long claws and talons.

18. Danäe was a beautiful maiden, the daughter of King Acrisius of

Argos. Jupiter fell in love with her and first appeared to her in a shower of golden rain. Perseus was born of this union.

19. Zeus visited Leda, the wife of Tyndareus, King of Sparta, in the form of a swan. She bore two eggs: from one issued Helen and from the other Castor and Pollux.

20. Zeus wooed Europa, the daughter of the king of Phoenicia, in the form of a bull. Three sons were born from this union: Minos, later king of Crete, Rhadamanthus, and Sarpedon.

21. The Holy Ghost, in Christian doctrine, is the third person of the trinity. He descended upon the Apostles at the first Pentecost, giving them the gift of tongues (Acts 2). The dove is his symbol. According to St. Matthew: "And Jesus, when he was baptized, went up straightaway out of the water: and lo, the heavens were opened upon him, and he saw the Spirit of God descending like a dove, and lighting upon him: and lo in a voice from heaven saying, This is my beloved son, in whom I am well pleased" (2:16–17).

22. It was the Archangel Gabriel (meaning "strength of God") who appeared to Daniel and who came to announce to the Virgin that she would give birth to Jesus (Luke 1:26).

23. See Jung, *Collected Works,* vol. 5 (New York: Pantheon Books, 1956), 433.

24. James George Frazer, *The Golden Bough* (New York: Criterion Books, 1959), 147, 139, 393.

25. Erich Neumann, *The Origins and History of Consciousness* (New York: Pantheon Books, 1954), 291.

26. See Jung, *Collected Works,* 5:97.

27. Ibid., 64.

28. Lionel Abel, "*Our Lady of the Flowers,*" *New York Review of Books,* 17 October 1963, 7–8.

Chapter Three

1. *Miracle de la Rose,* vol. 2 (Paris: Gallimard, 1951), 9; hereafter cited in the text as *M*.

2. Stewart, "Capefigue," 258.

3. See Jung, *Collected Works,* 5:412.

4. In this connection, it might be recalled that when Samson threw away the jawbone of the ass, God caused a fountain to gush forth, after which Samson's spirit was revived: "But God clave an hollow place that was in the jaw, and there came water thereout; and when he had drunk, his spirit came again, and he revived" (Judges 15:17).

5. It may be recalled that Jupiter's eagle had snatched the boy Ganymede away from Troy. Bulkaen, then, can be likened to Jupiter with his

symbolic bird of prey, and the narrator to the weak boy Ganymede unable to fight off the theft of his body and self.

6. Derrida, *Glas,* 60.

7. The character Harcamone was modeled on the young criminal Maurice Pilorge whom Genet so admired. Pilorge was a thief and a murderer who had spent forty days in prison with chains about his ankles and wrists' awaiting the guillotine and had been executed on 17 March 1939 at Saint-Brieux.

8. According to Jung, the capacity to make projections is a measure of one's inner potential. The fact that the narrator projected onto strong beings indicates that this inner potential was very great.

9. "L'Enfant criminel" (The child criminal was a speech Genet wrote in 1949 for broadcast on French radio. It was accepted by the station and then rejected. In this speech Genet spoke with profound emotion about the secret world of the juvenile delinquent.

Genet said that all criminals, himself included, reject and disdain society's pity. He and his fellow criminals are vindictive, angered at society, which seeks to "dull the cruel pain in the child's heart" by changing the name of penitentiary to reeducation center and by turning prison into a pleasant area. They want to be punished for their crimes.

To understand what prison life is about, "you have to have been that childhood, you have to have been that crime and sanctify it by a magnificent life, that is, the audacity, ruse, insolence . . . a taste for adventure against all rules of good." Young criminals wish to be punished for their crimes; they want prison to be a terrible hell. They want their lives to be heroic and audacious, perilous, and so beautiful. Genet would do his utmost to prevent those children from regaining "your houses, your factories, your schools, your laws, your sacraments." He wanted them "to violate them. . . ." To break, to destroy all that society stands for was Genet's goal. He had a mission, a battle to be won.

That Genet despised society, bore a grudge against it, and carried to the extreme Gide's words in *Les Nourritures terrestres,* "Families, I hate you," is obvious. If a criminal, however, repeats his fight and murders over and over again, he has become a completely negative force. The threat of being engulfed by society has become so much a fixation that the criminal is caught up in his own swelling sands. His crime or act, which might be considered heroic in the beginning, in the sense that it was audacious and required great courage to defy traditions, never passes beyond that stage. The criminal becomes identified with his crime and caught up in it, thereby turning it into a meaningless and destructive act.

That punishment for the juvenile criminal should "be worthy of the crime" is another requirement set by Genet. Such a rule is understandable, since it sets up another test the convict will have to pass to prove his heroism. The convict who seeks to prove his heroism over and over is like the revolutionary who wages his battle endlessly: though his blood may age his emotional development has remained that of an adolescent.

Genet had passed beyond the criminal stage but symbolically relived this period in his life over and over. Though he considered the criminal a hero and wanted him to break with society rather than return to it, Genet made his choice and returned to society. He lived a solitary and secluded life within his laws. His battle was now carried out on paper.

10. These four types—lawyer, judge, executioner, and chaplain—will again be characterized by Genet in future works.

11. The order was founded by Philip the Good, duke of Burgundy, in 1429.

Chapter Four

1. Philip Thody, *Jean Genet: A Study of his Novels and Plays* (London: Hamish Hamilton, 1969), 118.

2. Naish, *Genetic Approach,* 115.

3. Derrida, *Glas,* 107–8.

4. See Wilcocks, "Genet's Preoccupation with Language," 786.

5. *Pompes funèbres* (Paris: Gallimard, 1951), 107; hereafter cited in the text as *P*.

6. The French Maquis was an underground organization of patriots who fought to free France from German occupation during World War II.

7. The French Milice was an organization of French traitors who sided with the enemy during World War II.

8. F. Dostoevski, *The Brothers Karamazov* (New York: New American Library, 1962), 77.

9. See chap. 2, n. 9, for a definition of an archetype.

10. Neumann, *Origins and History of Consciousness,* 247.

Chapter Five

1. The plot of the clandestine edition of *Quarrel of Brest* varies slightly, but those variations will not be analyzed here. The phrase "amour contre nature" is translated as "love against nature" rather than "unnatural love" since it implies conflict, evoking Genet's real thoughts on the subject.

2. Anne of Brittany, 1477–1514.

3. *Querelle de Brest,* vol. 3 (Paris: Gallimard, 1953), 202; hereafter cited in the text as *Q*.

4. Saint Benoît-Joseph Labre (1748–83) was beatified in 1861.

5. Walter T. Stace, *Mysticism and Philosophy* (New York: Humanities Press, 1960), 9–29.

6. See Jung, *Collected Works,* vol. 11 (New York: Pantheon Books, 1963), 269.

7. Neumann, *Origins and History of Consciousness,* 121.
8. Choukri, *Jean Genet,* 31.
9. Ibid., 296.

Chapter Six

1. The commentators on Genet's theater have seen influences of Jarry, Artaud, Pirandello, Brecht, and Greek and Oriental theater. Genet's theater has been called symbolistic, realistic, surrealistic, and absurdist. Traces of all these dramatists and movements, and possibly more, appear in Genet's works. A discussion of such influences, however, as Genet might have undergone will not be taken up in this work.
2. Knapp, "Interview with Roger Blin," 113.
3. "Foreword to the New Edition of *The Maids,*" *Tulane Drama Review* (Spring 1963):37.
4. Ibid., 38.
5. Ibid., 39.
6. Knapp, "Interview with Roger Blin," 121.
7. Music for the ballet *'Adame Miroir* was composed by Darius Milhaud, with choreography by Mademoiselle Charrat. The ballet was danced by Roland Petit, Serge Ferrault, and Skouratof in 1949.
8. L. A. C. Dobrez, *The Existential and Its Exits* (New York: St. Martin's Press, 1986), 194.
9. *Le Funambule* (Décines: Isère, 1958), 179; hereafter cited in the text as *F*.
10. *L'Atelier d'Alberto Giacometti* (Decine: Isere, 1958), 9; hereafter cited in the text as *A*.
11. Jean Genet, *Oeuvres-complètes,* vol. 4 (Paris: Gallimard, 1968), 10.
12. Ibid., 26.
13. Derrida, *Glas,* 43.
14. Ibid., 44.

Chapter Seven

1. *The Maids and Deathwatch,* trans. Bernard Frechtman (New York: Grove Press, 1962), 161; hereafter cited in the text as *MD*.
2. Lucien Goldmann, "The Theatre of Genet: A Sociological Study," *Tulane Drama Review* (Winter 1968):53.
3. Genesis 12:1.
4. Matthew 10:34–36.
5. Maurice was perhaps modeled on one of Genet's lovers, Lucien Sénémaud, to whom he dedicated *Deathwatch*.
6. Neumann, *Origins and History of Consciousness,* 189–90.

7. This point, Jung indicates, is illustrated in Goethe's *Faust:* "Part of that power which would / Ever work evil, but engenders good!" (*Collected Works,* 5:234).

8. "She took the fruit thereof, and did eat, and gave also unto her husband with her; and he did eat" (Gen. 3:6).

9. "And the Lord said unto him, Therefore whosoever slayeth Cain, vengeance shall be taken on him sevenfold. . . . And Cain went out from the presence of the Lord, and dwelt in the land of Nod, on the east of Eden . . ." (Gen. 4:15–16).

Chapter Eight

1. Although *Deathwatch* was Genet's first play, it was produced after *The Maids,* in 1947.

2. Jacques Lacan, "Motif du crime paranoïaque: Le Crime des soeurs Papin," *Genet. Obliques* 2 (1972):100–103.

3. "A Note on Theatre," *Tulane Drama Review* (Spring 1963):37.

4. Jean-Paul Sartre, preface to *The Maids and Deathwatch,* trans. Frechtman, 7.

5. See Oreste F. Pucciani, "Tragedy, Genet and *The Maids,*" *Tulane Drama Review* (Spring 1963):42–59.

6. Jung, *Collected Works,* 5:327.

Chapter Nine

1. *The Balcony* was produced in Paris by Peter Brook at the Théâtre du Gymnase in May 1960. No cuts were made, and the play dragged. After the first performance, the scene of the revolutionaries was cut.

2. The action in *The Balcony* was so extraordinary that when I went to see this play and the theater caught fire, no one budged from their seats, so transfixed were they by the play. They thought the smoke and the flames part of the action. It was only some moments later, when the actors suddenly stopped and a man announced the fire, that the people began filing out of the theater but slowly—still not certain as to what was real and what was feigned.

3. Genet to Michael Breitman: "I have been the Victim of an Attempted Murder" (*The Theater of Jean Genet,* ed. Coe, 91).

4. Ibid.

5. Maria Shevtsova, "The Consumption of Empty Signs: Jean Genet's *The Balcony,*" *Modern Drama* (March 1987):36.

6. Johan Huizinga, *Homo Ludens: A Study of the Play Element in Culture,* quoted in Christiane V. Jacquemont, "The Essence of the Game and Its Locus in Jean Genet's *Le Balcon,*" *French Review* (December 1980):283–86.

7. *Cothurnus* or *cuthurn:* a high, thick-soled, laced boot worn by actors in Greek and Roman tragic drama.

8. *The Balcony,* trans. Bernard Frechtman (New York: Grove Press, 1960), 4; hereafter cited in the text as *B*.

9. See Gisèle Féal, *Le Balcon* de Genet ou le culte matriarchal: une interpretation mythique," *French Review* (April 1975):897–906; Neumann, *Origins and History of Consciousness,* 94.

10. Concerning mask identification: the actor portraying the television character Superman, George Reeves, committed suicide in real life because his audiences continually identified him with his character. Audiences were, in effect, murdering him, and he carried out their unconscious collective will by doing away with himself.

11. See Robert Brustein's excellent discussion of *The Balcony* in *The Theatre of Revolt* (Boston: Little, Brown, 1964), 394–402.

Chapter Ten

1. Pierre Démeron, "Conversation with Jean Genet," *Oui: For the Man of the World,* November 1972, 63–102.

2. Una Chaudhuri, "The Politics of Theater: Play, Deceit, and Threat in Genet's *The Blacks,*" *Modern Drama* (September 1985):366.

3. *The Blacks,* trans. Bernard Frechtman (New York: Grove Press, 1962), 12; hereafter cited in the text as *Bl.*

4. Knapp, "Interview with Roger Blin," 113.

5. Ibid., 117.

6. Ibid.

7. Even the names of the characters show the grotesqueness of Western-imposed culture on blacks: Archibald, Absalon Wellington; Dieu-Donné (God-given) Village; Miss Adelaïde Bobo (pain or a sore in child's language); Monsieur Edgar-Hélas (Alas) Ville (city) de Saint-Nazaire; Madame Augusta Neige (Snow); Madame Félicité Gueuse (Trollop, Tramp) Pardon: Mademoiselle Diop Etiennette-Vertu-Rose-Secrète. Sometimes the names are ironic in relation to the character of the person bearing them: Virtue, for example, is a prostitute; Snow is black. In the English translation some names were changed: Ville becomes Edgar Alas Newport News; Village becomes Deodatus Village.

8. Knapp, "An Interview with Roger Blin," 118.

9. Neumann, *Origins and History of Consciousness,* 178.

10. Felicity is the Black Queen. The conflict between the two actresses from Martinique who played the queens became so acute during the Parisian production that their hatred carried on offstage. Roger Blin said that the White Queen began burning incense to ward off the evil spell she had accused the Black Queen of casting upon her. The Black Queen, she said, had aimed the evil eye in her direction and had willed her to forget her lines. The Black

Queen's witchcraft was present in her stage actions, in her secret, symbolic, and ritualistic gestures. Strangely, the actresses had become completely identified with their roles.

Chapter Eleven

1. *Letters to Roger Blin,* trans. Richard Seaver (New York: Grove Press, 1969), 51; hereafter cited in the text as *L.*
2. Knapp, "Interview with Roger Blin," 119.
3. *The Screens,* trans. Bernard Frechtman (New York: Grove Press, 1962), 15; hereafter cited in the text as *S.*
4. Knapp, "Interview with Roger Blin," 118.

Selected Bibliography

PRIMARY SOURCES

Novels

Notre-Dame des fleurs. Monte Carlo, 1944. Translation: *Our Lady of the Flowers,* translated by Bernard Frechtman (New York: Bantam Books, 1964).

Miracle de la Rose. Lyons: l'Arbalète, 1946. Translation: *Miracle of the Rose,* translated by Bernard Frechtman (New York: Grove Press, 1966).

Querelle de Brest. N.p., n.d.

Pompes, funèbres. Bikini, 1947.

Plays

Les Bonnes. Lyons: l'Arbalète, 1947. 2d ed. *Revue l'Arbalète,* no. 12 (1948). Both versions: Sceaux: J.-P. Pauvert, 1954. Translation: *The Maids and Deathwatch,* translated by Bernard Frechtman (New York: Grove Press, 1962).

Haute Surveillance. Paris: Gallimard, 1947. Translation: *The Maids and Deathwatch,* translated by Bernard Frechtman (New York: Grove Press, 1962).

Le Balcon. Lyons: l'Arbalète, 1956. Rev. ed., 1960. Translation: *The Balcony,* translated by Bernard Frechtman (New York: Grove Press, 1960).

Les Negres. Lyons: l'Arbalète, 1958. Translation: *The Blacks,* translated by Bernard Frechtman (New York: Grove Press, 1962).

Les Paravents. Lyons: l'Arbalète, 1961. Translation: *The Screens,* translated by Bernard Frechtman (New York: Grove Press, 1962).

Poems

Chants secrets. Lyons: l'Arbalète, 1945.

Poèmes. Lyons: l'Arbalète, 1948; Décines, Isère, 1962.

Ballet

L'Enfant criminel and *'Adame Miroir.* Paris: Paul Morihien, 1949.

Essays, Letters, Etc.

L'Atelier d'Alberto Giacometti, Les Bonnes, L'Enfant criminel, Le Funambule. Lyons: L'Arbalète, 1958.

Lettres à Olga et Marc Barbezat. Lyons: L'Arbalète, 1988.

Lettres à Roger Blin. Paris: Gallimard, 1966. Translation: *Letters to Roger Blin: Reflections on the Theater,* translated by Richard Seaver. (New York: Grove Press, 1969).

Mademoiselle. Scenario, 1966.

Oeuvres complètes. 5 vols. Paris: Gallimard, 1951–79.

Autobiographical

Journal du voleur. Paris: Gallimard, 1948. Translation: *The Thief's Journal,* translated by Bernard Frechtman (New York: Grove Press, 1964).

Un Captif amoureux. Paris: Gallimard, 1986.

Interviews

Demeron, Pierre. "Conversation with Jean Genet." *Oui: For the Man of the World* 1, 2 (November 1972):63–102.

Fichte, Hubert. "Interview with Jean Genet: 'I Allow Myself to Revolt.' " Translated by Christa Dove. In *Critical Essays,* edited by P. Brook and J. Halpern, 178–90. Englewood Cliffs: Prentice-Hall, 1979.

Playboy, April 1964, 45–53.

SECONDARY SOURCES

Books

Bonnefoy, Claude. *Jean Genet.* Paris: Editions universitaires, 1965. Broad spectrum but limited approach to Genet's works.

Brooks, Peter, and Halpern, Joseph, editors. *Genet: A Collection of Critical Essays.* Englewood Cliffs, N.J.: Prentice-Hall, 1979. Helpful collection of essays on Genet's writings.

Cetta, Lewis T. *Profane Play, Ritual, and Jean Genet.* University: University of Alabama Press, 1974. Scholarly study.

Choukri, Mohamed. *Jean Genet in Tangier.* Translated by Paul Bowles. New York: Ecco Press, 1974. Brief insights on Genet the man.

Coe, Richard N. *The Vision of Jean Genet.* New York: Grove Press, 1968. Solid study of Genet's works.

Coe, Richard, N., editor. *The Theater of Jean Genet: A Casebook.* New York: Grove Press, 1970. Fine grouping of articles on Genet.

Derrida, Jacques. *Glas.* Translated by John P. Leavy, Jr., and Richard Rand. Lincoln: University of Nebraska Press, 1984. To be read only by those interested in Derrida's methodology.

Dichy, Albert et Fouché Pascal. *Jean Genet, essai de chronologie, 1910–1944.* CDN Bordeaux et la Différence, 1988. Well documented biography.

Driver, Tom F. *Jean Genet.* New York: Columbia University Press, 1966. Brief study.

Henning, Sylvie D. *Genet's Ritual Play.* Amsterdam: Rodopi, 1981. Well done approach to Genet's theater.

McMahon, Joseph H. *The Imagination of Jean Genet.* New Haven, Conn.: Yale University Press, 1963. Excellent early study of Genet's works.

Magnan, Jean-Marie. *Essai sur Jean Genet.* Paris: Seghers, 1966. Broad and insightful, but early study.

Moraly, Jean-Bernard. *Jean Genet, la vie écrite.* Paris: La Différence, 1988. Interesting and thoughtful biography.

Morris, Kelley, editor. *Genet/Ionesco: The Theatre of the Double.* New York: Bantam Books, 1969. Well done anthology.

Naish, Camille. *A Genetic Approach to Structures in the Works of Jean Genet.* Cambridge, Mass.: Harvard University Press, 1978. Pertinent and interesting study.

Obliques 2 (1972). Special issue on Genet. Insightful collection of essays on Genet's works.

Sartre, Jean-Paul. *Saint Genet: Actor and Martyr.* Translated by Bernard Frechtman. New York: George Braziller, 1963. A magnum opus.

Savona, Jeanette Laillou. *Jean Genet.* New York: Grove Press, 1984. Well done study of Genet's theater.

Thody, Philip. *Jean Genet: A Study of His Novels and Plays.* New York: Stein & Day, 1969. Early but insightful study of Genet's works.

Tulane Drama Review 7 (Spring 1963). Special issue on Genet and Ionesco. Innovative collection of essays on Genet.

Webb, Richard C., and Webb, Suzanne A. *Jean Genet and His Critics: An Annotated Bibliography 1943–1980.* Methuen, N.J.: Scarecrow, 1982. Invaluable bibliography.

Essays, Articles, and Sections of Books

Abel, Lionel. *Metatheatre: A New View of Dramatic Form.* New York: Hill & Wang, 1963, 76–82. Imaginative view of Genet's theater.

Aslan, Odette. "Genet, His Actors and Directors." Translated by Elaine Ancekewicz. In *Genet: A Collection of Critical Essays,* edited by Peter Brooks and Joseph Halpern, 146–55. Englewood Cliffs, N.J.: Prentice-Hall, 1979. Well done study.

Barthes, Roland. "Le Balcon: Mise en scene de Peter Brook au Theatre du Gymnase." *Obliques* 2 (1972):37–38. Interesting and imaginative approach.

Belli, Angela. "The Dramatic World of 'Saint' Genet." *Modern Language Studies* 10 (1980):36–40. Sensitive view of Genet's theater.

Bermel, Albert. "Society as a Brothel: Genet's Satire in *The Balcony.*" *Modern Drama* 19 (1976):265–80. An added insight to Genet's *The Balcony.*

Borie, Monqique. "Genet's ou le cérémonial-simulacre et l'irréalisation des mythologies." In *Mythe et théâtre aujourd'hui: Une Quête impossible? Beckett, Genet, Grotowski, le Living Theatre.* Paris: Nizet, 1981, 69–116. Well done and helpful comparisons.

Brustein, Robert. *The Theatre of Revolt.* Boston: Little, Brown, 1964, 361–411. Fascinating chapter on Genet's theater and Artaud's influence on it.

Chaudhuri, Una. "The Politics of Theater: Play, Deceit, and Threat in Genet's *The Blacks.*" *Modern Drama* 28 (1985):362–76. An added dimension to *The Blacks.*

Curtis, Jerry L. "The World Is a Stage: Sartre versus Genet." *Modern Drama* 17 (1974):33–41. New explications of the Sartre/Genet dichotomy.

Dobrez, L. A. C. *The Existential and Its Exits.* New York: St Martin's Press, 1986, 195–257, 281–92. Thoughtful and excellently researched study.

Dort, Bernard. "Genet et Pirandello ou d'un théâtre de la representation." *Lendemain* 19 (1980):73–83. A serious comparison between the two authors.

Esslen, Martin. *The Theatre of the Absurd.* Garden City, N.Y.: Doubleday, 1961, 140–97. Excellent but brief study of Genet's theater.

Féal, Gisèle. "*Le Balcon* de Genet ou le culte matriarcal: Une Interpretation mythique." *French Review* 48 (April 1975):897–907. Excellent and well written approach.

Federman, Raymond. "Genet: The Theatre of Hate." Translated by Frank Abetti. In *Genet: A Collection of Critical Essays,* edited by Peter Brooks and Joseph Halpern, 129–45. Englewood Cliffs, N.J.: Prentice-Hall, 1979. Well worth perusing.

Goldmann, Lucien. "Une pièce réaliste: *Le Balcon* de Genet." *Les Temps Modernes* (June 1960):1885–96. Political view.

———. "The Theater of Genet: A Sociological Study." *Drama Review* 12 (Winter 1968):51–62. An interesting sociological view.

Graham-White, Anthony, "Jean Genet and the Psychology of Colonialism." *Comparative Drama* 4 (1970):208–15. Well done article.

Guicharnaud, Jacques. *Modern French Theater from Giraudoux to Beckett.* Revised edition. New Haven, Conn.: Yale University Press, 1967, 259–76. Informative section on Genet's theater.

Innes, Christopher. *Holy Theatre: Ritual and the Avant-garde.* Cambridge: Cambridge University Press, 1981. Sensitive and profound study.

Jacquemont, Christiane V. "The Essence of the Game and Its Locus in Jean Genet's *Le Balcon.*" *French Review* 53 (1980):282–87. Penetrating study of the game element in *The Balcony.*

Knapp, Bettina L. "An Interview with Roger Blin." *Tulane Drama Review* 7 (1963):111–26. First interview of its kind. Sheds new light on Genet's theatrical works.

Kott, Jan. "The Icon and the Absurd." *Drama Review* 14 (1969):17–24. Excellent article on Genet's theater.

Magnien, Victor, *Les mystères d'Eleusis.* Paris, 1950. Fascinating and enriching study of the mysteries in ancient Greece.

Millet, Kate. "The Balance of Power." *Partisan Review* 2 (1970):199–218. New insights at the time.

Nelson, Benjamin. "*The Balcony* and Parisian Existentialism." *Tulane Drama Review* T19 (Spring 1963):60–79. Pertinent philosophical explication.

Pronko, Leonard. *Avant-Garde: The Experimental Theater in France.* Berkeley: University of California Press, 1962, 140–53. Excellent work.

Pucciani, Oreste F. "Tragedy, Genet and *The Maids.*" *Tulane Drama Review* T19 (Spring 1963):42–59. Impressive study of *The Maids.*

Scarborough, Margaret. "The Radical Idealism of *The Screens.*" *Modern Drama* 15 (1961):355–68. Incisive work on *The Screens.*

Schechner, Richard. "Genet's *The Balcony:* A Perspective on a 1979–80 Production." *Modern Drama* 25 (1982):82–104. A penetrating view of *The Balcony* from a production point of view.

Scherzer, Dina. "Les Appellatifs dans *Le Balcon* de Genet." *French Review* 48 (1974):95–107.

———. "Frames and Metacommunication in Genet's *The Balcony.*" In *Semiotics of Drama and Theatre,* edited by Herta Schmid and Aloysius Van Kesteren, 368–92. Amsterdam: John Benjamins Publishing Company, 1984. Serious semiotic studies of Genet's theater.

Shevtsova, Maria. "The Consumption of Empty Signs: Jean Genet's *The Balcony.*" *Modern Drama* 30 (1987):35–45. Incisive approach to the visual elements in Genet's *The Balcony.*

Stewart, Harry E. "A Note on Verbal Play in Genet's *Le Balcon. Contemporary Literature* 10 (1969):389–95.

———. "Capefigue: An Historical Source for Jean Genet's Fantasies." *Romance Notes* 22 (1982):254–58.

———. "In Defense of Lefranc as a 'Hero' of *Haute Surveillance,*" *French Review* 45 (1971):365–72.

———. "The Case of the Lilac Murders: Jean Genet's *Haute Surveillance.*" *French Review* 48 (1974):87–94.

———. "Jean Genet: Bogus Count of Tillancourt." *French Review* 50 (1977):724–31. Excellent article on various aspects of Genet's theater.

Taubes, Susan. "The White Mask Falls." *Tulane Drama Review* 7 (1963):85–92. One of the earliest and best studies of *The Blacks.*

Todorov, Tzetan, *Poétique.* Paris: Seuil, 1968. Penetrating study of a personal view poetics.

Walker, David H. "Revolution and Revisions in Genet's *Le Balcon.*" *Modern Language Review* 79 (1984):817–30. Serious and sensitive study.

Wilcocks, Robert. "Genet's Preoccupation with Language." *Modern Language Review* 65 (1970):785–92. One of the best analyses of Genet's use of language.

Witt, Mary Ann Frese, "Spatial Narration in Jean Genet's *Notre-Dame-des-fleurs* and *Le Balcon.*" In *Myths and Realities of Contemporary French Theater: Comparative Views.* Lubbock, Texas: Texas Tech Press, 1985. Serious study of some of Genet's works.

Yale French Studies 29 (Spring–Summer 1962). Special issue devoted to "The New Dramatists." An excellent overall but early view.

Other Works

Artaud, Antonin. *Oeuvres complètes.* Vols. 1–14. Paris: Gallimard, 1956–79. A must for a better understanding of Genet.

Bergler, Edmund. *Homosexuality: Disease or Way of Life.* New York: Hill & Wang, 1956. Important for a better knowledge of the homosexual's psyche.

Foucault, Michel. *Discipline and Punish, The Birth of the Prison.* Translated by C. Alan Sheridan. New York: Vintage Books, 1977. Significant study on French prisons.

Frazer, Sir James George. *The New Golden Bough.* Edited, with notes, by Theodor H. Gaster. New York: Criterion Books, 1959. Most important work for a broader understanding of Genet's religious views.

Huinziga, Johan, *Homo Ludens: A Study of the Play Element in Culture.* New York: Roy Publishers, 1950. Important for a better understanding of the play element and its ramifications in Genet's writings.

Jung, C. G. *Collected Works.* Vols. 1–20. Princeton: Princeton University Press, 1957–79. Important for a psychological understanding of Genet's novels, plays, and essays.

Kerenyi, C. *The Gods of the Greeks.* New York: Grove Press, 1960. Interesting background material.

Neumann, Erich. *The Origins and History of Consciousness.* New York: Pantheon Books, 1954. Important study on the notion of the hero and of men's groups.

Stace, Walter T., *Mysticism and Philosophy.* New York: Humanities Press, 1960. Important for insights on Genet's brand of mysticism.

Index